IN THE NAME OF ALLAH, THE BENEFICIENT, THE MOST MERCIFUL

Dialogue With An Atheist

Dr. Mostafa Mahmoud

© Dar Al Taqwa Ltd. 1994

Second Edition March 2000

ISBN 1 870582 09 8

All rights reserved. No part of this publication may be reproduced, stored in a retrieval system, or transmitted, in any form or by any means, electronic, mechanical, photocopying, recording or otherwise, without the prior permission of the publishers.

Translated by Mohamed Yehia

Published by:
Dar Al Taqwa Ltd.
7A Melcombe Street
Baker Street
London NW1 6AE
email : dar.altaqwa@btinternet.com

Printed and Bound by :
De-Luxe Printers
245a, Acton Lane, Park Royal,
London NW10 7NR
website : http://www.de-luxe.com
email : de-luxe@talk21.com   (for AppleMac files) or
        printers@de-luxe.com (for Pc windows files)

CONTENTS

		Page
I.	He Begot None, Nor Was He Begotten	5
II.	"If God Preordained My Deeds, Why Should He Judge Me?"	11
III.	Why Did God Create Evil?	23
IV.	"What About Those Unreached By The Quran?"	29
V.	Paradise and Hell	37
VI.	Is Religion An Opium?	45
VII.	Islam and Women	61
VIII.	The Spirit	71
IX.	The Conscience	83
X.	Is Pilgrimage A Pagan Rite?	87
XI.	Could Muhammad Be The Author of The Quran?	91
XII.	The Quran Did Not Come From A Human	113
XIII.	Doubts	125
XIV.	Religion and Evolution	137
XV.	"There Is No God But Allah"	149
XVI.	K.H.Y. 'A.S.	155
XVII.	The Miracle	163
XVIII.	The Meaning of Religion	169
XIX.	"We Won Worldly Happiness And You Got Delusions"	175

I
He Begot None, Nor Was He Begotten

My friend is a man who likes to argue and delights in talking. He thinks that we, naive believers as we are, feed on illusions and miss the pleasures and attractions of this world beguiling ourselves with Paradise and the Houris. He studied in France where he got a Ph.D. degree, consorted with Hippies, and came to disbelieve in everything.

He adressed me sarcastically:

— You say that God exists. The chief among your proofs is the law of causation which stipulates that every artefact, creature, or existent must have been brought into being by a maker, creator, or efficient cause: a piece of fabric points to the weaver, a painting to the painter, an engraving to the engraver. The universe, according to this logic, is the most cogent proof of a Puissant God who created it.

Granted that we believe in this creator, aren't we entitled, according to the same logic, to ask, "Who created the Creator; who created that God you talk about?" Doesn't your own reasoning and in keeping with the same law of causation lead you to this question? Now, What have you to say about this dilemma?

I replied to him by making clear that his question was meaningless.

– There is no dilemma or anything of that sort. You grant that God is a Creator and then you ask about who created Him making Him both creator and created in the same sentence, which is a contradiction.

The other side of your question's meaninglessness is that you imagine the creator as being subject to the laws which govern his creatures. Causation is a law for us who live in space and time. God, who created space and time, is necessarily transcendent in relation to both and it is an error on our part to think that he is bound either by them or by their laws. It is God who created the law of causation and we cannot consider Him as subject to the law He created.

In this sophistry of yours you are like those dolls that, seeing they move by springs, imagine that the human who made them must also derive his motion from the action of springs. If they were told that he is self-moved, they would retort that it is impossible for anything to move spontaneously since everything in their world is moved by a spring. Just like them, you cannot imagine that God exists in His own Essence with no need of an efficient cause; and this is because you see everything around you in need of such a cause. It is as if you thought that God needs a parachute to descend among men or a fast car to reach His prophets; God is infinitely exalted above such conceptions.

The German philosopher, Immanuel Kant realized, in his **Critique of Pure Reason,** that the mind cannot comprehend infinite realities and that it is by nature fitted only to apprehend particulars. It is incapable of apprehending such a universal or total existence as that of the divinity. God was known by conscience not by reason. Just as our thirst for water is a proof that it exists, our yearning for justice is proof to us that a just Being exists.

Aristotle followed the chain of causality tracing the chair from wood, wood from the tree, the tree from a seed, and the seed from the planter. He had to conclude that this chain which regresses into infinite time must have begun with an 'uncaused' cause, **a primum mobile** in no need of a mover, a creator who has not been created. This is the same thing we assert of God.

From another quarter, Ibn Arabi, the muslim mystic, replied to the question as to who made the creator by saying that it can only occur to a disordered mind. According to him, it is God that substantiates existence and it would be erroneous to point to existence or the universe as a proof of God. This is the same as saying that light indicates day and it would be a lopsided argument to claim that day proves the existence of light.

God says in a Divine Utterance (Hadith Qudsi): "It is I who aids in proving and finding, there is no proof leading to me."

God is the proof which is in no need of another proof. He is the self-evident Truth; and He is the evidence that substantiates everything. He is manifest in order, precision, beauty, and regularity; in tree leaves, in the feathers of a fawn, in the wings of the butterfly, in the fragrance of flowers, in the chanting of the nightingale, in the harmony of planets and stars which makes up that symphonic poem we call the universe. If we allege that all this came into being by chance, we would be like a person who believes that blowing-up the types of a press into space can result in their spontaneous assembly into an authorless Shakepearean sonnet.

The Quran spares us all these arguments with a few, expressive words. It says without sophistry and in a decisive clarity:

> "Say that God is One, the Eternal.
> He begot none nor was he begotten.
> None is equal to Him."

* * *

My friend continued to question me in his sarcastic tone: "Why do you say that God is one? Why shouldn't there be many gods sharing the 'work' among themselves?"

I chose to reply to him not with the aid of the Quran but with the logic he accepts: that of science. My answer was that God is one because the entire universe is built out of one material and according to a unified plan. The ninety two elements in the Mendelev table are built from hydrogen and in the same manner in which stars and suns flame-up in space; namely, by fusion and the emission of atomic energy.

All forms of life are built of carbon composites – they are all charred when burned – according to one anatomical plan. An anatomy of a frog, a rabbit, a pigeon, a crocodile, a giraffe, and a whale reveals the same anatomical structure in all. The same arteries, veins, cardiac chambers, and bones correspond in all of them. The wing of the pigeon is the fore-leg in the frog: the same bones with only a slight transformation. The long neck of the giraffe contains seven vertebrae, we find the same number in the hedgehog's neck. The nervous system in all consists of the brain, the spinal cord, and the motor and sensory nerves. Their digestive apparatus contains the stomach, the duodenum, and the small and large intestines, The genital apparatus has the same components: the ovary, the uterus, the testicles and their ducts; while the urinary system in all consists of the kidney, the uriter, and the bladder. The anatomical unit in each of these creatures is the cell. Whether we are dealing with plants, animals, or humans, we meet with the same features; they all breathe, breed, die, and are born in the same way.

What is so strange, then, in asserting that the creator is one? Does He suffer from a deficiency to need completion? It is the imperfect only who multiply. If there were more than one god, they would fall among themselves, each taking his own creation to his side and the world would be ruined. To God is sublimity and compelling – attributes which brook no associates.

* * *

My friend mocked the concept of divinity (**Robobyya**) that we entertain. He wondered at that god who interfered in every thing big or small mastering all creatures and "intimating to the bees to abide in mountains". No leaf falls but He knows of it and no fruit grows out of its bud but He takes count of it. No female conceives and gives birth without His knowledge. It is He who causes the foot to stumble over a hole and the fly to fall in a plate of food. Even if the phone is dead or the rain doesn't fall or, conversely, if it pours down, He is behind all these events. "Don't you keep your god busy", asked my friend, "with too many trivial things under such conception of Him as that?"

I don't really understand my friend. Would god, in his opinion, be more of a divinity if He relieved himself of all responsibility and, turning his back to the world he created, left it unattended to destroy itself in conflicts? Is the true divinity in his estimation that idle, unconscious being who does not hear, see, or respond to his creatures and look after them? It is to be further asked: from what quarter did he know that certain affairs are important and serious enough to so deserve such attention?

The fly, which appeared to the enquirer so insignificant that it doesn't matter whether it falls in a plate of food or not, can change history with such an unimportant fall. It could thus infect an army with cholera giving victory to the other side and, consequently, totally altering the course of history. Wasn't Alexander the Great killed by a mosquito? The most trivial premises can lead to the most serious consequences, whereas the most important beginnings can issue in nothing. The Knower of the Unseen alone realizes the value of everything.

It remains to be asked whether my friend has set himself up as a trustee over God defining his prerogatives for Him; our Lord is most Holy and High above such a naive conception. The God worthy of divinity is He whose Knowledge comprehends all; Who misses not one atom either in earth or sky.

He is God, the All-Hearing, the Responder, the Mindful of His creatures.

II

'If God Preordained My Deeds, Why Should He Judge Me?'

My friend spoke gloatingly thinking that his arguments would hold me captive by the scruff of my neck.

– You say, he argued, that God manages everything in this creation with fate and predestination and that he has preordained our deeds. If this applies to me, for instance, in the sense that all my actions have been preordained by him, why then should I be accountable before him? Don't give me the usual reply that choices are open before me. Nothing is more preposterous than this lie. Let me ask you: have I had any choice in my birth, sex, height and build of body, colour, and country? Do I choose that the sun rise and the moon set? Is it by my choice that a blow of fate descends on me, that death surprises me, or that I can only escape from a pitfall of calamity by committing crime? Why should God force me to do a certain deed and then hold me responsible for it?

'If you argue that I am free and that I have a will besides that of God wouldn't that be considered a kind of polytheism since you are led to admit the multiplicity of wills? Moreover, what can you say to counter the ideas of historical materialism concerning the determinism of environment and circumstances as well as the various forms of 'inevitabilities' that adherents of that philosophy advocate?

– Having blurted out these words like bullets, my friend breathed in relief thinking that I have been completely vanquished and that he had only to shroud my creed before the burial. I, however, began to speak in a quiet voice:

You are victim to certain fallacies. Your deeds are foreknown to God in His Record but they are not preordained for you against your will. They are only preordained in His Prescience just as you may foresee, in the light of your knowledge, that your son will commit fornication and he actually goes on to do it. Have you compelled him to it? Or was it, in fact, a foreknowledge which came true because founded on your comprehension of the situation?

Another confusion you fall in is your description of the freedom of the will as a lie arguing that you had no say in determining your birth, sex, height, colour, or country and that you cannot will the sun to move from its orb. The cause of the confusion is that you conceive freedom differently than we, the believers, see it. You have **absolute** freedom in mind; therefore, you ask whether you can have a choice in making yourself white or black, tall or short or whether you can will to move the sun form its place or stop it in its orbit. Hence, you enquire plaintively, "Where is my freedom?"

You are, in fact, talking about absolute freedom, the freedom to do as you will in the universe – such a kind of freedom is God's alone. We do not hold this view of freedom as we are guided by the Quranic verse:

> "Your Lord creates what He will and chooses freely, but you have no power to choose."
>
> **The Story,** 68

No one has any choice in matters relating to creation because it is God who creates what He wills and pleases. He will not hold you responsible for your short or admonish you for your long stature, nor will He punish you for failing to stop the sun in its orbit.

The sphere of accountability is the area of **Taklif** or Divine Injunction. Within this area you are free and your argument should be confined inside its compass. You are free to repress your appetites, to bridle your rage, to resist the promptings of your ego, to deter your evil intentions, to enhance your benevolent tendencies.

> You can be generous with your money and self.
> You can tell the truth or lie.
> You can restrain your hand from forbidden gains.
> You can divert your eye from prying into the sensitive spots of others.
> You can hold your tongue and refrain from cursing, back-biting, and slander.

In this area we are free; and it is in this area that we are liable to account and questioning.

The freedom we should be discussing is relative and not absolute; it is man's freedom within the sphere of **Taklif** or Injunction. This latter kind of freedom is real and the evidence for its reality is our innate, intuitive sense of it. We feel responsibility and contrition for our wrong-doing and we feel relief over our good deeds. We sense in every moment of our lives that we are involved in weighing and choosing from among several possibilities. The primary function of our mind, indeed, is to choose and favour from among alternatives.

We clearly and decisevely distinguish between the trembling of our hand as a result of fever and its movement as it writes a letter describing that trembling. We are conscious of the shivering as determined and compulsory and of the letter-writing as free and voluntary. If we were compelled or conditioned in both cases we wouldn't be able to make the distinction. This freedom is further affirmed by our experience that it is impossible under any pressure to compel the heart to accept anything it does not want to. You can force a woman with threats and beating to undress but no pressure whatsoever can make her love you with all her heart. This indicates that God has safeguarded our hearts from all forms of compulsion and duress and that he created them free. This is why God judges according to what the heart harbours and the intentions bear. The believer who is forced to utter expressions of **Shirk** (polytheism) or blasphemy under threatening or torture will not be held accountable for them as long as his heart is steadfast in faith. In the following verse God absolves such person of responsibility:

> "Those who are forced to recant while
> their hearts remain loyal to the faith
> shall be absolved."
> **The Bee,** 106

A further element of confusion in connection with the question of freedom of will is that some people understand human freedom as meaning a transcendence of Divine Will and a management of affairs independent of God. Consequently, they accuse the advocates of freedom with

Shirk (polytheism) and with setting up equals to God who bid and dispense like Him. This view, my friend, is what you echoed in your talk about the multiplicity of wills. It is a mistaken conception; for human will does not transcend Divine Will. Man, in his freedom, may act contrary to what satisfies God, but he cannot do anything in contradiction to His Will. God granted us freedom to transgress against His wishes (we disobey Him) but He gave none the freedom to transcend His Will. In fact, we encounter here another facet of the relative nature of human freedom.

All our actions are within the sphere of Divine Will and are subservient to it even if they go against God's wishes and violate the **shari'a** (religious law). Our freedom itself is a divine gift that God willingly bestowed and it was not forcefully extorted from Him. Indeed, our freedom is exactly what He willed; and this is how we can understand this Quranic verse:

> "You cannot will but by the will of God."
>
> **Man,** 30

Our will is subservient to His; it is a grant from Him, a gift of His Kindness and Generosity. It lies within His own Will; there is no duality, opposition, or competition between our wills and God's Will and Judgment.

Understanding freedom in this way does not go against **Tawhid** (faith in the Oneness of God) or sets up equals to God who bid and dispense like Him. Our freedom is precisely what He wills and decides.

A third point of confusion about the issue of freedom is that some people who tackled the question of fate and predestination or the controversy of determinism versus freedom have understood fate as a compelling of man to that which is contrary to his nature and bent. This is an error into which you have also fallen, my friend; God has unequivocally denied that He resorts to compulsion:

> "If we will, we can reveal to them a sign from heaven before which they will bow their heads in utter humility."
> **The Poets,** 4

The meaning here is clear enough: God could have compelled men to believe by revealing incontestable signs (**ayat**) or miracles but He did not choose this path because compulsion is not one of His laws:

> "There shall be no compulsion in religion. True guidance is now distinct from error."
> **The Cow,** 256

> "Had your Lord pleased, all the people of the earth would have believed in Him. Would you then force faith upon men?"
> **Jonah,** 99

Compulsion, it is plain, is not part of Divine Law.

Fate and predestination should not be conceived as a forcing of people to what is against their natures; on the contrary, God destines each human being to a fate which corresponds to his intentions – He wills him to what he himself really wills and He desires for him what he himself desires. There is no duality here. God's preordination is identical to the creature's freedom of choice because God predestines every man according to his own desires and intentions:

> "Whoever seeks the harvest of the world to come, to him We will give in great abundance; and whoever desires the harvest of this world, a share of it shall be his."
> **The Counsel,** 10

> "There is a sickness in their hearts which God has increased,"
> **The Cow,** 10

> "As for those who follow the right path, God will increase their guidance."
> **Muhammad,** 17

In the Quran, God addresses the captives of war thus:

> "If God finds goodness in your hearts, He will give you that which is better than what has been taken from you,"
> **The Spoils,** 70

God preordains according to the intentions and heart of man: if these are evil, man will come to evil; if good, good will be his fate. There is no duality or opposition; predestination is freedom of choice as God predestines us to what we choose with our hearts and intentions. There is no injustice, compulsion, or duress in this regard and there is no subjection to what is against our natures:

> "For him that gives in charity and

guards himself against evil and believes in goodness, we shall smooth the path of salvation; but for him that neither gives nor takes and disbelieves in goodness, We shall smooth the path of affliction."

The Night Journey, 5–10

"It was not you who smote them; God smote them."

The Spoils, 17

The last verse indicates that the strike effected by man and that preordained by God merge into one and the same strike. This is the solution to the puzzle of fate and predestination: man is to intend while God is to enable and dispose, good for good and evil for evil.

Human freedom is not a fixed sum but a relative potential which is capable of increase. Man can enhance his freedom with knowledge. By inventing tools, instruments, and means of transportation, he has managed to traverse our planet, to defeat distance, and to overcome the limitations of time and space. Through study of the laws of environment, he could control and exploit it for his benefit; he knew how to resist heat, cold, and darkness thus compounding his freedom in the sphere of action.

Knowledge, thus, has been one means of breaking bounds and restraints and of unshackling freedom. Another means to those ends has been religion: invoking God's aid by taking the path leading to Him and receiving Revelation, support, and guidance from Him. This was the way of the prophets and their followers. Solomon utilized the jinn, mastered the winds, and spoke with birds by God's aid and gifts. Moses parted the sea while Christ raised the dead, walked on the water, and healed the blind-born, the leper, and the sightless. We read about the **Walis** (men of God) and the blessed for whom the 'terrain is folded' and the unseen made known. They attain to these levels of freedom by perseverance in God's worship and by endearing themselves to Him. He responds by endowing them with emanations of His hidden knowledge. Once again we encounter knowledge but this time it is **Ladduni** knowledge (one peculiar to God).

Abu Hamed El-Ghazali sums up and solves the problem of freedom and predestination in two sentences: Man has freedom of choice in relation to what he knows, he is preordained with regard to what he knows not. El-Ghazali means that the more knowledgeable man becomes the freer he is – and this holds true whether the knowledge meant is objective (Worldly) or **Ladduni,** coming from God alone.

* * *

Materialistic thinkers commit a grievous error when they conceive man as prisoner to historical and class determinism thus turning him into a link in a chain of economic and social laws and movements from which he cannot escape or extricate himself. Man becomes, in their view, a straw blown about helplessly in a violent air-current with no aid to steer himself with.

The phrase they tirelessly invoke as if it were a natural law is "the inevitability of class conflict." According to scientific analysis, this is a fallacy since there are no inevitabilities in the human sphere but, at best, there are only probabilities and expectations. Indeed, the distinction between man and physical objects, machines, or cogs resides in this fact. Whereas solar eclipses can be accurately predicted to the minute and second and the sun's future movements known for days and years, no one can know what is hidden in a man's intentions or what he will do the next day and the day after. Such human factors can only be known in the form of probabilities or likely causes of action provided, of course, that enough information is at hand to aid in shaping the relevant judgments.

All the prophecies of Karl Marx, for instance, have proven wrong: communism did not arise in an advanced country, as he predicted, but in a backward one. The conflict between capitalism and communism did not intensify but both camps were led by **rapprochement** to a state of "peaceful co-existence". Communist countries have even gone so far as to open their doors before American capital. The sharpening of contradictions that Marx expected to occur in the capitalist society leading to its bankruptcy did not materialize; on the contrary, the capitalist economy flourished while discord and dissention spread among the members of the socialist camp.

Marx's calculations were mistaken in their entirety proving the error of his deterministic system. The 'history-moving' conflict of our age is that non-class confrontation between the Soviet Union and China and not the class struggle proclaimed by Marx as the **leitmotiv** of his system. All this indicates the failure of materialistic thinking to understand man and history and the error of its predictions about the future. The failure resulted from a basic fallacy; namely, the materialistic conception of man as a fly caught in a net of inevitabilities and the total disregard of the reality of man's freedom.

There are, still, the materialists' arguments about the conditioning of man by the environment, society, and circumstances. Man, it is claimed, does not live alone and his freedom is not practiced in a vacuum. In reply to these arguments we say that the influence of the environment, society, and circumstances as factors antagonistic to human freedom confirms the dialectic nature of that freedom and does not negate it. The freedom of the individual can only assert its existence in the face of an opposing force seeking to displace it. If man moves in a vacuum where no resistance of any kind exists, he will not be free in the logical meaning of the word since there will be no obstacles for him to overcome and thereby manifest and emphasize his freedom.

III

Why Did God Create Evil?

My friend resumed his arguing in a derisive note of voice.

– How dare you speak of your God as the Perfect, the Omnipotent, the Merciful, the Bounteous, and the Ruthful while He is the creator of all evils in the world: disease, old age, death, earthquakes, volcanoes, microbes, poison, scorching heat, freezing cold, and the torments of cancer that spare neither new-born babe nor decrepit senile. If God is truly Love, Beauty, and Goodness, how then did it come that He created hatred, ugliness, and evil?

– This problem, raised by my friend, is among the basic questions of philosophy; opinions differed and schools of thought split over it. We say that God is all mercy and goodness. He did not enjoin evil but suffered its existence for a wise end:

> "God does not enjoin what is indecent. Do you tell of God that you do not know? Say: My Lord ordered you to act in justice. Turn to Him wherever you kneel in prayer and call on Him with true devotion".
>
> **The Heights,** 28

God only enjoins justice, amity, charity, forbearance, and benevolence. He only accepts what is good. Why, then, does

He suffer the unjust, the murderous, and the thieving to perpetrate their deeds? The answer is that He wanted us to be free; freedom necessitates error; it would be meaningless if it did not allow us the right to trial, error, and right judgment and the unrestricted choice between sin and obedience.

God was quite capable of making us all benevolent by compelling us to obey him. This, however, would have entailed that He deprive us of the freedom to choose. But in His Plan and Law, freedom with suffering is more honourable to man than slavery with happiness. That is why He let us sin, suffer, and learn; this is the wisdom in His sufferance of evil to exist.

Nevertheless, a just and objective consideration of the matter would reveal to us that benevolence is the rule in the universe while evil is the exception. Health is the rule, disease the exception; we spend most of our life enjoying health and are visited by sickness only for a few days in comparison. Similarly, a total of the times during which earthquakes have struck would amount to only a handful of minutes in relation to the age of our planet which is measured in many millions of years. In the same reckoning, volcano eruptions or wars are but short-lived convulsions in the life of nations interrupting long periods of quiet and peace.

Moreover, we can discern a benevolent aspect in almost everything. Sickness bequeathes immunity; suffering engenders hardiness, fortitude, and endurance; earthquakes relieve the pent-up pressures inside the earth preventing its crust from blowing-up and restoring mountains to their places as 'belts' and 'weights' that stabilize the crust; volcanoes spew up minerals and other hidden resources thus covering the land with rich soil; wars unify and amalgamate nations leading to their gathering in blocks and alliances and then in a League of Nations and, finally, in a Security Council which is like a universal tribunal where complaints are aired and settled. The greatest inventions were made during wars; peniciline, atomic power, rockets, jet planes and many others came out of the crucible of war. The ancient wisdom still holds true: "Out of the snake's poison comes the antidote." Even now we manufacture the serum from the microbe. If our forefathers have not met their death we would not have attained the positions we now hold. Evil in the universe is like the shaded spaces in a painting; if you come very near to the painting, you will see these parts as defects and faults in it; but if you draw back to a distance and take a general view of the painting as a whole, you will discover that the shades are necessary and indispensable fulfilling an aesthetic function within the structure of that artwork.

Could it be possible for us to know health if disease did not occur? Health glitters as a crown on our heads that is only known when we are ill. Likewise, it is impossible to know beauty but for ugliness or to know that which is normal without getting acquainted with the abnormal. This is why the philosopher Abu Hamed El-Ghazali said that the universe's imperfections are the essence of its perfection just as the curving shape of the bow is the essential feature of its usefulness since 'a straight-shaped bow' would be unfit for shooting arrows.

Another use of hardships and sufferings is that they sort out men and reveal their true nature. As an Arabic verse eloquently put it:

"But for hardships all men would rule supreme. Bounty beggars and boldness kills."

These tribulations are trials by which we know ourselves; they are tests which determine our degrees in the sight of God.

This world is but one act of a play that has many; death is not the end of the story but its beginning. It is inadmissible to judge a play on the testimony of just one act or to reject a book because its first page did not appeal to us. The judgment in both cases is incomplete. The entire significance of any such work can only be known at its end.

One wonders at the alternative that our scoffing friend has in mind. Does he, for instance, envisage for us a life without death, sickness, senility, defeciencies, disability, grief, or suffering? Is he seeking absolute perfection? But that latter is for God alone. The really perfect being is one and cannot be many. Indeed, why should he multiply? What can he possibly lack in himself to seek for it in others? The upshot is that my friend will not be satisfied except by becoming God which is presumption **par excellence.**

Let us, in our turn, mock him and those, like him, who scoff at everything. We ask those who dream of our life becoming a flawless paradise, 'What have you done to deserve a paradise on earth?' Indeed, what services did our friend render to humanity so as to set himself up as God, the One and the Vanquisher Who orders everything to be and creates all by His **fiat?**

My grandmother had more sense than our French-educated, 'learned' friend. She used to say in all simplicity: 'Good comes from God, evil from ourselves.' A terse remark, indeed, but what a true view of the entire matter is contained here in a nutshell! God sends the winds and makes the river flow but a greedy captain may overload his ship with people and goods and when it sinks, he curses fate and destiny. What is God's fault here? He sent a benevolent wind and caused the river to flow smoothly but greed and avarice turned this good into evil.

Indeed, what beautiful and fine words: 'Good comes from God, evil from ourselves'.

IV

What About Those Unreached By The Quran?

My learned friend started to scratch the top of his head. He was, evidently, thinking hard to find a pitfall that would finish me off this time. He began to speak slowly and deliberately:

Very well, what can you tell me about the fate of a person whom the Quran or, for that matter, any other revelation or prophet did not reach? What fault can you lay at him? What, in your creed, will be his fate on the Day of Judgment? I have in mind, for example, an Eskimo in far away polar regions or a negro deep in the jungle. What will befall such a person at the hands of your God on Doomsday?

–I began my answer to him at once:

Let me, first of all, correct your view of the issue involved here. You have based your questions on a false premise. God informed us in the Quran that He deprived no one of His Mercy, Revelation, Words, or Signs:

> "For there is no nation that has not been warned by a messenger."
> **Fater,** 24

> "We raised a messenger in every nation."
> **The Bee,** 36

The prophets mentioned in the Quran are not all whom

God sent. There are thousands of others about whom we know nothing. Concerning those messengers, God says to his prophet Muhammad:

> "Of some you have already heard, of
> others we have told you nothing."
> **The Forgiver,** 78

God, in fact, sends intimations to everything; to bees, for instance:

> "Your God inspired the bees, saying:
> 'Build your homes in the mountains,
> in the trees, and in the thatchings men make."
> **The Bee,** 68

This inspiration may be a Revelation, a Book delivered by Gabriel, or an illumination caused by God in a person's heart. It can be a state of 'relief' in mental disposition, an insight into truth, or an understanding of things. Again, it can take the shape of reverence towards and fear of God as well as an attitude of piety. Indeed, no one that ever 'tunes up' his heart and sense will be deprived from receiving a favour from God. Those, however, who block their ears and hearts will not benefit from any number of books, messengers, or miracles.

God says that he blesses whomever He wills of his creatures with His mercy and that He is accountable before none for His deeds. For a wisdom known only to Him, He may send warnings to some but not to others so that these latter may be excused in His sight and the slightest indication of faith accepted from them.

We can really never know. A mere fearful glance at the sky

by that primitive negro may be more redeeming with God and acceptable to Him than our prayers. Nevertheless, a closer consideration of the creeds of such primitive negroes reveals that they had messengers and revelations like our own. We know, for instance, that the Mau Mau tribe believes in a God it calls 'Mogabe' and describes him as a single being that was neither begotten nor begets and that has no equal or like. This divinity is invisible and only known by his deeds and effects. He is a creator, a donor of livelihood, a bestower, and a compassionate being who heals the sick, relieves the distressed, sends the rain down, and hears prayers. According to tribal lore, lightning is that deity's dagger and thunder the sound of his footfall.

Isn't this 'Mogabe' almost the same as our own God? From what quarter did those tribesmen receive such conception unless a messenger and a revelation came to them at some period of their history? As usual, this message must, with the passage of time, have fallen victim to superstitions that corrupted its original purity.

We similarly know that the Niam Niam people believe in a single divinity they call 'Mbole' who, according to their sayings, moves everything in the jungle, visits the evildoers with thunderbolts, and rewards the virtuous with livelihood, blessing, and security. The Shilock tribe, we also know, believes in Jok, a single deity whom they describe as both invisible and manifest. He abides in the sky and everywhere and he is the creator of everything. The Denkas believe in a single God, Nialok, whose name literally means 'he who is in the sky' or the sublime. By what name other than Islam can we call such creeds? What else can they be but messages delivered by prophets who came to those peoples?

> "Believers, Jews, Christians, and Sabaeans – whoever believes in God and the Last Day and does what is right – shall be rewarded by their Lord; they have nothing to fear or to regret."
>
> **The Cow, 62**

Even the Sabaeans (or those among them who worshipped the sun as one of God's signs and believed in the Oneness of God, in resurrection, in Judgment, and performing good deeds) will have their wages from God.

It is well-known that God's mercy varies in how it is bestowed. There are those born blind and others who enjoy sight. Some have lived in the age of Moses and saw him with their own eyes parting the sea with his staff; others have lived in the time of Jesus and witnessed how he raised the dead. As for us, we only know of these miracles by hearing about them. Receiving a report of something is surely not equal to seeing it with the eye; for to see is other than to hear of a certain event. Nevertheless, belief and disbelief do not hinge upon miracles. Obdurate non-believers witness wonders from the prophets sent to guide them but have no more to say of these miracles than describing them as 'fabricated sorcery'.

It is certain that our learned friend, who has just returned from France, has known three Books – the Torah, the Bible, and the Quran – in his own language. These Revelations, it seems, only exacerbated his indulgence in disputation. To evade the entire subject he shifted the discussion to a hypothetical primitive in the jungle unreached by any revelation and went on to ask us the following question:

"Why does God's mercy vary? Why should God reveal his signs to some while others know of them only through reports?"

We reply to him by observing that revealing miracles to some may not be a blessing but a temptation. For didn't God warn the companions of Christ who asked for a table to descend among them from heaven?

> "God said: 'I am sending one to you. But whoever of you disbelieves hereafter shall be punished as no man has ever been punished."
>
> **The Table,** 115

The reason for this warning is that the coming of miracles is always accompanied by an increase in the severity of punishment for those who disbelieve after seeing them. Happy indeed are those who believe from hearing of revelation without witnessing any miracles. And woe to those who see them but persist in disbelieving.

The Quran you have with you is a witness against you and a warning for you. On the Day of Reckoning it will not be a mercy but the contrary. Sparing the Eskimo of the polar regions such an irrefutable witness may be a sign of mercy, pardon, and alleviation on the Day of Judgment. A look at the sky from this ignorant Eskimo even once in his life may be sufficient for God to accept him as a sincere believer.

As for the reason why God shows more mercy to some than to others, it is a dispensation he bases upon his knowledge of hearts:

> "He knew what was in their hearts. Therefore He sent down peace upon

them and rewarded them with a speedy victory."

Victory, 18

God's knowledge of us and of our hearts precedes our creation in the wombs; it goes back to when we were spirits around His Throne. Some of us were attracted to His Light and were completely absorbed in it, while others directed their attention away from Him to enjoy the spectacle of the universe **(malakoot)** shunning the splendour of their Creator. Ever since that time immemorial the latter have deserved the lower degree and were predestined to perdition. Thus said those who 'see' **(Ahl el-Moshahada).**

What we experience in our short life on earth is not everything that there is. Knowing the wisdom behind every suffering and privation is something that belongs only to the Omniscient. If I were asked why God created the pig in that shape we know, I can only reply that God chose for it a 'piggish' form becuse its nature or 'self' is swinish. It was right and just that this animal be created in that shape we are familiar with.

All the dispensations we see around us are just but realizing the all-encompassing wisdom and discovering that hidden justice is a task that is not within our ken. It is for this that the Last Day was decreed; when the "scales" will be set up and the Omniscient tell us of everything we disputed about.

And now, my friend, I shall set your heart to rest with the decisive argument in this question. God said in His Book that He will punish only those whom He warned beforehand through His messengers:

"Nor do We punish a nation until We

have sent forth a messenger to warn them."

The Night Journey, 15

Have I thus quietened your fears? Allow me further to add that the most peculiar aspect of your questions in this connection is their deceptive pretense of belief and pity for the poor negro deprived of the light, mercy, and guidance of the Quran. In truth, they indicate your disbelief in the Quran or its light and guidance. They are designed more for inveiglement and subterfuge. They run contrary to your own inner conviction and I can only decribe this attitude as perversity in its quintessence. You are endeavouring to persuade us of an argument of which you personally do not have any proof. Don't you agree with me that your reasoning is in need of mending?

V
Paradise and Hell

My learned friend was perfectly sure of himself as he delivered his bombshell in slowly-pronounced but strongly-stressed words:

– How is it that God, the Compassionate and Merciful, punishes us for a transgression committed in a moment of finite time with eternal and infinite torment – 'In Hell they dwell forever'? Who are we and what is our worth in comparison to God's greatness to deserve such vengeance? Man is only an atom or a speck of dust in the universe and relative to God's Majesty he is infinitely more insignificant than that – he is, in fact, **nothing** in the full meaning of this word.

– Our learned friend's conceptions are in obvious need of correction.

We are not like atoms or specks of dust in the universe. Our standing in the sight of God is not insignificant but considerable. Didn't He breathe in us of His Spirit? Didn't He command the angels to bow for us? Didn't He promise us the inheritance of the earth and the heavens? Didn't He say of us:

> "We have bestowed blessings on Adam's Children and carried them over land and sea. We have provided

> them with good things and exalted them above many of Our creatures."
>
> **The Night Journey,** 70

We have, then, something of God's Spirit in us. Nor are we atoms or specks of dust in relation to the universe. If we consider our bodies only we may well be like grains in the wide, spacious world. But don't we contain this universe in and comprehend it with our minds realizing its laws and defining the orbits of its planets and stars? The astronauts who landed on the moon ascertained that all our calculations and designs have been true and accurate. Doesn't this indicate that in so far as our spirit is concerned we are larger than the universe and that we 'contain' it? The Arab poet was right when he spoke of man in the well-known verse:

> You deem yourself a tiny body
> While the great world is within you contained.

Man, as the sufis say, is the comprehensive book while the entire universe is but some of its pages.

Man, then, is of great standing and importance. He comes from the Spirit of God. His deeds necessitate accountability. As for the finite sin in time for which God visits us with infinte torment in eternity, this is simply another fallacy of my friend's – the self-confident Ph.D.! God speaks about those immortalized in Hell-fire who beg to be returned to earthly life so as to change their deeds to the better:

> "But if they were sent back, they would return to that which they have been forbidden. They are liars all".
>
> **Cattle,** 28

Their guilt, according to this verse, is not confined to one moment of time. It is, in fact, a permanent feature of their make up that repeats itself at any time. Indeed, if they were returned to a new life they will commit the same transgressions all over again; therefore, they lie in their promise of improvement. Their sinning is an innate and enduring attribute of their psyche and not a momentary slip in the context of some exceptional life circumstance.

In another Quranic verse, God describes those inveterate sinners:

> "On the day when God restores them all to life, they will swear to Him as they now swear to you, thinking that they have some standing. Surely they are liars all."
>
> **She That Disputeth,** 18.

This is a flagrant form of perversity and impudence which motivated them to lie even to God and to swear falsely before Him on that Day of the Great Stand when veils are lifted and covers are removed; indeed, this is most audacious and overbearing.

We are definitely not dealing with a transgression limited to a point in time but one that continues through time and after time itself has ended. We are really confronting a psyche that carries within itself its eternal evil. Hence, everlasting torment is only equitable for such souls. The Quran candidly puts it: 'but (they) shall never come out of Hell.' (The Cow, 167). Ibn 'Arabi says that mercy for those souls lies in their habituation to Hell-fire which will become their appropriate abode through infinite ions.

There is undoubtedly an affinity of element between certain transgressing souls and fire; some of these souls are in reality blazes of envy, grudging, voluptuousness, jealousy, and bitterness; they are flames of wrath, resentment, rebellion, and other animal passions that flare and rage as a veritable fire. Such souls can never live at peace or endure just one hour without causing conflict and setting fire to everything that surrounds them; for fire is their element and natural habitat. It is a just judgment that Hell be their final abiding place. It will be like placing a thing in its rightful element. If they were admitted to Paradise they would not be able to enjoy it. Didn't they disdain peace while on earth?

We ought to be broad-minded in our conception of either Hell or Paradise. Hell-fire in the other world is not a 'grill' and what goes on there is not burning in its earthly sense. God says that the damned in Hell-fire speak with and curse each other. Hell has in its midst a tree with 'fruit': the Zaqoum Tree which grows from the bottom of Gehena. In Hell there is also scorching water for the tormented to drink of. Such place where a certain kind of tree and of water exist and where the damned talk must be another sort of fire than the one we know:

> "As it enters every nation will curse the one that went before it, and when all are gathered there, the last of them will say of the first: 'There, Lord, are the men who led us astray. Let their punishment be doubled in Hell-fire".
> **The Heights,** 37–8

The tormented talk while **in** Hell-fire; a fire 'whose fuel is men and stones' (The Cow, 24).

This fire, then, is something that belongs to the Unseen (**Gaib**); all references to it can be taken as symbolic. It must not, however, be understood that we deny physical torment advocating, instead, a 'psychic' punishment. Physical torment is so clearly indicated that no one dare contest or doubt it. We certainly believe in its occurrence. What we suggest is only that the nature and particulars of such torment as well as the qualities and features of the Hell-fire mentioned belong to the hidden **Gaib** or Unseen. As it seems from Quranic references, it is a fire unlike that we know in our world just as the bodies exposed to it will be different from the frail, clayey bodies we now have.

The same view can apply to Paradise. It is not a market display of vegetables, dates, pomegranates, and grapes. These Quranic descriptions of it are mere symbols, approximations, or illustrations that bring its truth within the conceptual compass of human minds:

> "This is a similitude of Paradise which the righteous have been promised. There shall flow in it rivers of unpolluted waters, and rivers of milk for ever fresh."
> **Muhammad,** 15

In my understanding of the first sentence of this verse God is only giving our minds an approximation of heaven; but the true details of heavenly bliss remain in the Unseen:

> "No mortal knows what bliss is in store for them as a reward for their labours."
> **The Prostration,** 17

> "A Paradise as vast as heaven and earth."
>
> **The Imrans,** 133

Paradise cannot be a mere garden. Its fruits are abundant, 'unforbidden, never-ending' (The Event, 32); they are certainly unlike our own earthly fruits which can be forbidden and which cease from season to season. The wine of Paradise 'will neither pain their heads nor take away their reason', it is, undoubtedly, very much different from the wine known to us which leaves a hangover and unsettles the mind. The Quran goes on to say that God 'shall take away all hatred' from the souls of the blessed in Paradise (The Heights, 43). Here again we confront an unknown means of purifying hearts.

Paradise, then, is just like Hell: a matter belonging to the Unseen. This view does not, nevertheleles, imply any denial of physical bliss. We believe that Paradise contains both physical and spiritual bliss just as Hell is physical and spiritual torment at one and the same time. What we would rather emphasize is that the details and nature of such bliss or torment are unknown to us, that Paradise is not just a fruit and vegetable market nor is Hell an oven for baking meat.

Torments in the hereafter are not a form of tyranny God exercises over his creatures but a kind of purification, enlightenment, correction, and mercy:

> "And why should God punish you if you render thanks to Him and truly believe in Him?"
>
> **Women,** 147

Men were not all predestined for torment when they were created. God does not punish the believer who has knowledge of Him; He only visits His torment on the obdurate disbeliever with whom all means of guidance and acquainting with the faith and all explanations of it have failed:

> "But We will inflict on them the lighter punishment of this world before the supreme punishment of the world to come, so that they may return to the right path,"
>
> **The Prostration,** 21

It is God's law that these men should taste the minor punishments of this world to be roused from their torpor and frightened out of their deafness and slumber 'so that they may return to the right path.'

If all such approaches fail, with the disbeliever persisting in his attitude, there remains only one option open: to inflict the promised torments on him so that he may come to know the **truth.** Acquaintance with the truth is the essence of mercy. Should God neglect those obstinate disbelievers in their blindness and ignorance, He would be unjust – far removed is He from this. To be led to Hell-fire is a kind of **Care** for such benighted souls. All God's actions are merciful. He shows the mercy of correction and of enlightenment to the benighted in Hell; and He is merciful with his generosity and blessings to the knowing in Paradise:

> "I will visit my scourge upon whom I please: yet my mercy encompasses all things".
>
> **The Heights,** 156

God encompassed everything with his mercy even those under punishment.

Let us, in our turn, ask our learned friend: Would God, in your opinion, be more just if He treated both sinners and sinned against, murderers and murdered in the same manner throwing up a tea-party for all on the Last Day? Is justice, in our friend's view, synonymous to equalling black with white? To those that find it impossible for God to inflict punishment we may say: Doesn't He actually inflict suffering on us in this world? Aren't old age, sickness, cancer... etc. basic forms of torment? Who created the microbe? Aren't these all warnings that we are dealing with a God who **can** torment?

VI

Is Religion An Opium?

My learned friend continued his argument with a significant look in his eyes:

– What do you say to counter those who describe religion as an opium which drugs the poor and oppressed and makes them acquiesce in the injustice and destitution they suffer under, leaving them to dream of Paradise and the Houris while the rich hold tight to their wealth as a right incumbent from God's creation of men in various 'degrees'?

What, further, can you say in reply to those who believe that religion did not really descend from God but, rather, originated from the 'earth' springing from social causes and conditions to be employed as a weapon by one class against another?

– My friend was, of course, referring in his last sentence to the materialists and their ideas. I pointed to him that nothing can be more erroneous than describing religion as an opium. In its essence, religion implies burdens, injunctions, and responsibilities; it surely does not mean disencumberment or disavowal of anything and is, thus, no shirking of responsibility and no opium. Our religion stresses work and not laziness:

"Say: 'Act' God will behold your

works, and so will His Prophet and the faithful;"

Repentance, 105

We believe in true reliance upon God (**Tawakkul**) not in helpless inaction (**Tawakul**). Reliance upon God necessitates resolve, expenditure of every possible effort, exhaustion of every energy and means, and, then, submission to God's will and fate: 'When you are resolved, put your trust in God', (The Imrans, 159). Resolve comes first. The Prophet's advice to the man who wanted to leave his she-camel untied relying upon God's preserving of it was: "Tie it and rely on God"; that is, he should do his best to secure the animal and then put his trust in God.

Religion means watchfulness, attentiveness, alertness, self-questioning, and the heeding of conscience in every deed, word, or prompting – this is not the way of opium-eaters. The true opium-eater is the materialist who rejects religion because he wants to escape its consequences and responsibilities and who thinks that the moments he lives belong to him so that he goes about doing as he likes believing that there is no watcher, questioner, or resurrection after death. How can a man like this compare with the true muslim who considers himself responsible even for his 'seventh neighbour' and who blames himself if any individual in his nation starves or if any animal is mistreated feeling that he has not fulfilled a duty made incumbent on him by his religion.

It is also not true that our religion originated from 'the soil', from social conditions and causes, to be employed as a weapon in the hand of one class against another and to perpetuate the wealth of the rich and the poverty of the poor. Quite the opposite is true. Islam came as a revolt against the rich, the money-hoarders, the exploiters, and the oppressors. It expressly enjoined that wealth should not be monopolized and exchanged among the rich alone but it should be open for all as a right:

> "Proclaim a woeful punishment to those that hoard up gold and silver and do not spend it in God's service."
>
> **Repentance,** 340

'Spending' starts with the compulsory Zakat (payable on various sorts of income and assets) of $2\frac{1}{2}\%$. It can go up, voluntarily, to include all you have in your pocket or at hand leaving yourself only with your daily sustenance:

> "They ask you what they should give in alms. Say:
> 'What you can spare.'"
>
> **The Cow,** 219

That which can be spared is anything more than is required for sustenance and the satisfaction of needs.

In this way, Islam combined the compulsory, legal injunction with an exhortation to conscience and free will. This is more honourable for man than forceful confiscation and expropriation. Islam gradated the ceiling for spending in charity up to ninety per cent of income but at the same time it did not lay down any compulsion. Islam was not revealed to confirm injustice but to declare an unconditional revolt against all the unjust. It came as a sword waging war on tyrants and dictators.

The materialists, however, quote verses from the Quran such as the following to charge that religion is reactionary and class-oriented:

"To some of you God has given more than to others."
The Bee, 71

"We have exalted some in rank above others."
Ornament, 32

In reply to such charge we can say that these verses apply to modern London, Paris, Berlin, or Moscow just as much as they apply to Cairo, Damascus, or Jeddah. If we survey the streets of Moscow, for example, we shall find some people walking on their feet, some riding bicycles, some driving a Moskovitch, and yet others being driven in a luxurious Zim car. What else can this be but an expression of variance in livelihood itself, in ranks, and in economic levels?

The existence of differences between people is an axiomatic fact. Communism has not been able to level such differences. Even extremist advocates of materialism and anarchy did not call for equality. Equality as such is impossible; for how can we make two originally unequal people the same? From the moment of birth, men are unequal in intelligence, strength, beauty, or talents. They are born in ranks or degrees in more ways than one. The utmost that economic philosophies have aspired to is to achieve equality in opportunities and not equality of men, to secure for everyone the same opportunity in education, health-care, and a minimum standard of living – the same things, in fact, that religion calls for. To abolish degrees and differences would not only be injustice in quintessence but a contradiction to nature as well. The natural order as a whole is based on variance, differentiation, and variety in everything: in the fruits of the earth, in animals, and in men. In cotton we find short and long stapled varieties as well as such Egyptian types with local names like 'Gizeh 7', 'Sclarides', or 'Fully Good Fair'. We know several varieties of Egyptian dates – the yellow Samani, the red Zagloul, and the Hayyani – and of grapes such as the Banati, the Fayyoumi, and the Smyrna. In animals and men, the ranks, degrees, or variations are found in a far greater measure.

Differentiation, in fact, is the law of existence as a whole. The wisdom behind it is quite clear. If all men were born with the same bodies, features, and qualities there would have been no need for them to be created in the first place. It would have been sufficient for just one 'prototype-man' to be created **in lieu** of the rest. This would have naturally been generalized to every order of existence leading to the impoverishment and bankruptcy of creation. The wealth and fertility of nature show only in the variety of its yields and fruits and in the differences among its products.

Nevertheless, religion did not stand passively in the face of such variance between rich and poor. It instructed that this condition be rectified and described it as a temptation and trial: "We test you by means of one another. Will you not have patience?" (The Criterion, 20). We, as men, shall discover how the powerful, for instance, uses his strength: will he help the weak or employ it to strike, murder, and tyrannize? We shall see how the richman manages his wealth: will he dominate and squander or sympathize and be charitable? We shall also find out how the destitute behaves in his poverty: will he envy and grudge, steal and embezzle or will he work and toil at his best possible capacities to raise his standard of living in a manner that is lawful and just?

Religion commanded justice, the redress of wrongs, and

equality of opportunities. It raised the torments of the hereafter as a threat saying that there will be more widely-spaced ranks or degrees in the next world to redress what has not been rectified in this:

> "See how we have exalted some above others. Yet this life to come has greater degrees and is more exalted."
>
> **The Night Journey,** 21

To those who accuse Islam of political reaction we reply that it brought with it the most progressive principles of rule. Respect for the individual has reached its summit in Islam which not only preceded but excelled the Human Rights Declaration in this regard. An individual, in the consideration of Islam, is equal to humanity in its entirety:

> "Whoever killed a human being, except as a punishment for murder or other wicked crimes, should be looked upon as though he had killed all mankind; and whoever saved a human life should be regarded as though he had saved all mankind."
>
> **The Table,** 32

All material achievements and reforms or the construction of dams and factories cannot balance the murder of just one individual at the hand of the ruler in the process of carrying out these reforms; it would be as if the ruler, in committing this crime, has killed all humanity.

Such is a zenith in the respect for individuals which has not been attained by any political doctrine old or new. In Islam, the individual has an absolute value whereas his value in all other political philosophies is relative. Under Islamic injunctions he is secure in his home, in his private affairs ('there shall be no spying and back-biting'), and in his wealth, income, possessions, and freedom. Everything has a place in the Quran: the exchange of greetings, making room for those sitting in a gathering, and the utterance of kind words.

The Quran forbade oppression, tyranny, and the monopoly of power by any one individual. God told the Prophet, perfect and competent as he was, 'You are not a compeller over them.' (Qaf, 45). God also said to His Prophet:

> "Therefore give warning. Your duty is only to remind them. You are not their ward."
>
> **The Overwhelming, 21**

> "The believers are a band of brothers."
>
> **The Chambers, 10**

The Quran also forbade the worship of rulers and the deification of the great:

> "None of us shall set up mortals as gods besides Him,"
>
> **The Imrans, 64**

> "Your Lord has enjoined you to worship none but Him,"
>
> **The Night Journey, 23**

God prohibited demagoguery, the flattery of the mob and the riff-raff, and compliance with the misleading majority:

> "Most men do not know (that God has power over all things)."
>
> **Joseph, 21**

> "But most of them are senseless men."
>
> **The Spider, 63**

> "Most men do not believe (in the Day of Doom),"
>
> **The Forgiver, 59**

> "They (the greater part of mankind) follow nothing but idle fancies and they do but utter falsehood,"
>
> **Cattle, 116**

> "They are like the cattle – nay, they are farther astray."
>
> **The Criterion, 44**

God similarly enjoined against racialism and discrimination on its basis:

> "The noblest of you in God's sight is he who fears Him most"
>
> **The Chambers, 13**

> "It was He who created you from a
> single soul."
>
> **The Heights,** 189

Islam is, in a scientific sense, a dialectical synthesis of the materialistic bent of Judaism and the spirituality of Christianity; it combines that strict, dry justice which laid down the taking of an eye for an eye and a tooth for a tooth with the amiability and excessive toleration which preach the turning of the left cheek. The Quran came as a golden mean between the Torah, which has been corrupted to become a purely materialistic book with no mention of the Judgment Day, and the Bible, which inclined to total asceticism. The Quran lays down the law of mercy which incorporates both justice and love. It allows the legitimacy of self-defense but prefers pardon, forbearance, and forgiveness:

> "And whoso is patient and forgives –
> that, verily, is of the steadfast heart of
> things."
>
> **Counsel,** 43

Whereas capitalism gave the individual free rein in the pursuit of profit to the extent of exploiting others and while communism completely crushed any freedom in that sphere, Islam offered the golden mean:

> "Unto men a share of that which they
> have earned, and unto women a share
> of that which they have earned."
>
> **Women,** 32

The individual is free to acquire gains but he cannot keep them all to himself; he has a right only to a share of them. The poor have a share in such gains which is to be taken in the form of the compulsory Zakat portion of $2^1/_2\%$ or in voluntary charitable spending of up to ninety per cent of income. This share is not given by way of alms or, indeed, charity but it represents God's right in the gains. It was through such fine balance that Islam preserved both the individual's freedom and the right of the poor.

The Quran perfectly hits the mark when it records God's call to the nation (Ummah) of Islam: 'We have made you a middle nation;' (The Cow, 143). Islam has chosen the just mean with regard to everything. It is not a mathematically determined mean but rather a dialectical or synthetic structure which incorporates thesis and antithesis – the right and the left – transcending and adding to them. It cannot, therefore, be claimed that there is either a rightist or a leftist tendency in Islam; there is only the Sirat (Path) of the moderate mean which we call 'the Straight Path'. Any inclination either to the right or to the left of this path is a deviation from Islam.

The Quran did not tie us down to a definite political programme or a detailed system of government for God knew, in his Prescience, that circumstances change necessitating **Ijtihad** or inventive intellectual effort to formulate different programmes for different ages. In this way, the muslim would be free to effect an exchange with the branches of knowledge available at every age without being confined to a set and unchanging programme. That is why the Quran found it sufficient to proclaim the above-mentioned general political recommendations as the essentials of ideal government. It did not shackle us with a dogmatic theory and this is, in fact, one of the aspects of its miraculous nature and not a defect or shortcoming.

In this approach we find another fact of the Quran's idea of progress which antedated all other doctrines of progress. We answer those alleging that religion means rigidity and petrification by pointing out that Islam was never a creed of that sort; it always called for and championed thinking, contemplation, development, and change. Consider, for example, such verses in their clear indications:

> "Say: 'Travel in the land and see how He originated creation,"
> **The Spider, 20**

> "Let man consider from what he is created. He is created from a gushing fluid that issued from between the loins and the ribs."
> **The Morning Star, 7**

> "Will they not reflect on the camels and how they were created; and heaven and how it was raised on high; the mountains and how they were set up, the earth and how it was levelled flat."
> **The Overwhelming, 17–19**

All these are unambiguous commands for investigating the creation of man, the animals, the mountains, the strata of the earth's crust, and space with its stars and orbits. Such investigations, in fact, encompass all the material we now group under disciplines such as geology, astronomy, anatomy, physiology, biology, and embriology.

We have, then, in the Quran clear injunctions to travel through earth gathering evidence, deducing laws, and understanding how its creation was begun. This is what is called today the science of evolution.

There is no taboo against error. Islam rewards any one who expends an intellectual effort and errs; it doubles that reward to him who hits on the truth.

There is no foundation to the charge that belief in religion is the cause of our backwardness while atheism is the secret behind the progress of the west. What is true is that we lagged behind when we turned our backs to the teachings of our religion. When the muslims did adhere to the injunctions of their creed there was real progress, a nation that extended from the Atlantic Ocean to the Persian Gulf, and scholars like Ibn Sina in medicine, Ibn Rushd in philosophy, Ibn el-Haytham in mathematics, Ibn el-Nafis in anatomy, and Gaber Ibn Hayyan in chemistry.

Nations at that time received knowledge from us. European dictionaries still keep the Arabic names of many stars and constellations. The French word for the distilling device, **imbique,** and the verb for that process, imbiquer, still retain their Arabic original: **Ambeeq.**

The west did not advance by atheism but through science. The roots of the entire mistaken notion go back to the clerical tyranny of the Middle Ages, to the Inquisition's restrictions against science and scientists exemplified by Galileo's imprisoment and Giordano Bruno's burning at the stake.

When the Church ruled supreme and was diverted by the Popes from its noble mission, it became a force for backwardness. Superficial critics imagined that such a situation applies to Islam as well. This is a mistake; Islam does not institute any clergy or papacy. God did not set up any mediators or warders between Him and the believers. When Islam actually ruled it was a factor of progress as we indicated and as history testifies belying such shallow allegations.

Unequivocal Quranic verses incite to knowledge and enjoin its acquisition; they do not set up any opposition between religion and science:

> "Say: 'Lord increase my knowledge."
> **Taha,** 114

> "Are those who know equal with those who know not?"
> **The Troops,**

> "God bears witness that there is no god but Him, and so do the angels and the men of learning."
> **The Imrans,** 18

In the last verse God even couples the men of learning with the angels relating both to the honour of His name and His act of witnessing.

The very first word revealed of the Quran was "Read"; the knowledgeable are promised the highest ranks:

> "God will raise to high ranks those that have faith and knowledge among you."
> **She That Disputeth,** 11

The word 'knowledge' and its various derivatives recur in the Quran about eight hundred and fifty times. How can anyone, in the light of the previous remarks, speak about a contradiction between religion and science or about restrictions imposed by the former on the latter?

Studying religion and deepening its understanding is a desirable attitude. The entire history of Islam is nothing but continuous movements of revival and development. The Quran is certainly innocent of imposing any rigidity on men. Everything in our religion accepts development except, of course, the essence of its creed and the core of its Shari'a (Law). God is one and He will not 'develop' to become two or three; His status is absolute. Similarly, evil will remain evil while good remains so. Murder will never become a virtue nor will theft change into a blessing or lying metamorphose into an ornament for the good. Apart from these elements, religion is open before thinking, intellectual assays, additions, and development.

Islam, in its quintessence, is rationalistic. It accepts dialogue and argument and encourages the use of mind and reasoning. In more places than one we find the Quran asking rhetorically: 'Don't they reason?', 'Don't they understand?'. The believers are described as the 'people of reason' and the Quran tells us:

> "The meanest beasts in God's sight are those that are deaf, dumb, and devoid of sense."
> **The Spoils,** 22

> "Have they never journeyed in the land? Have they no hearts to reason with, or ears to hear with?"
> **The Pilgrimage,** 46

Respect for the mind is the heart and essence of religion, positive attitudes its core, and revolution its spirit. Islam has never been a negative creed of submission:

"Fight for the sake of God those that fight against you,"

The Cow, 190

"God loves those who fight in His cause in ranks as if they were a solid structure."

The Ranks, 4

At the very centre of our religion we encounter values such as sacrificing the self, wealth, and sons in the struggle for God's cause. Steadfastness in fighting and the express injunction against turning tail are Islamic values; and so are endurance, constant readiness, and the defeating of despair.

How can a religion with such high regard for flexibility, rationalism, the scientific approach, and positive and revolutionary attitudes be libelled by charges of rigidity and petrification except from the tongues of such men as my 'dear', learned friend who, although just back from France with his doctor's degree, is ignorant of the rudimentaries of his own religion and has not even read one letterr of its Book: the Holy Quran?

VII

Islam and Women

My learned friend began the discussion by asking me:

– Don't you agree with me that Islam's attitude towards women is reactionary?

He, then, took to counting the proofs of his charge: Polygamy, seclusion at home, the veil, man's monopoly of the right to divorce, man's right to beat and desert his wife's bed, the issue of intercourse with the slave-girls 'you may own', man's famous 'authority' (**Kowama**) over his wife, and, finally, the favouring of males with a double share compared to that of females when inheritances are distributed.

Trying to recollect myself after this outburst by my friend, I began to address him:

– The charges this time are many needing lengthy replies. Let us, however, begin at the beginning – before Islam. I think you know perfectly well that Islam was revealed in the midst of a **Jahili** (barbaric and heathen) environment which condemned new-born girls to be buried alive while allowing men to marry up to twenty women and to force their slave-girls to prostitution and keep the 'proceeds' to themselves. Islam's licence for men to marry up to four wives was, in effect, a kind of restriction not of abandon. Its teachings saved women from death, servitude, humiliation, and the stigma of shame.

Are European women in a happier lot now amid the prevailing sexual 'permissiveness' and the extra-marital relations that plague most marriages? Wouldn't it be more honourable for a woman to become a second wife to a person she loves and enjoy all the rights and respect of matrimony rather than to be a secret mistress stealing pleasure behind closed doors?

In Islam, however, polygamy is only a **license** almost impossible to be utilized because it is conditional upon a proviso very difficult to fulfill:

> "But if you fear that you cannot maintain equality among them (the wives) marry only one."
> **Women,** 3

> "Try as you may, you cannot treat all your wives impartially."
> **Women,** 129

God, thus, makes it clear that even the most scrupulous will not be able to treat his wives equally. The only men who can fulfill this proviso, those who are really super-conscientious, are the prophets, the 'men of God', and those who follow their path.

As for the charge of seclusion, it concerns the Prophet's wives who, as the supreme ideals, were enjoined by God to 'stay in your homes' (The Clans, 33). This is an indication that the ideal position for woman is to be a mother and a housewife completely devoted to her home and children. We can imagine the state of a nation whose women are in the streets and offices while the children are sent to orphanages and nurseries. Would such a nation be in a better condition than one whose women are devoted mothers and housewives and where the children are brought up under their mothers' attention and in well-cared for families? The answer is quite obvious.

Islam, however, is quite aware and tolerant of the reasons that oblige women to go out of their homes and seek work. There were women jurisprudents and poetesses throughout the periods of Islamic history. Women went out to war and for study. The injunction to stay at home was addressed to the Prophet's wives, as we said, in the sense that they were higher examples. There are several and separate levels for the ideal, the possible, and the actual. The Prophet's wives accompanied him in his battles, this entails that going forth to aid the husband in an honourable struggle is a blameless affair.

As for the veil **(Hijab),** it is in women's favour. Islam permitted them to reveal their faces and hands (up to the wrists) and enjoined the covering of all other parts of their bodies. It is well known that what is forbidden is always desired and that concealment of alluring features enhances their attractiveness. On account of total nudity among primitive tribes, the sexual passion of the males lapses into abeyance with the lack of curiosity. A man in such tribes will only have intercourse with his wife once a month and if she becomes pregnant, he does not come near her for two years.

When naked 'flesh' abounds on beaches in summer and is available for oggling eyes, the bare body loses its lure, novelty, and charm becoming an ordinary spectacle that arouses no curiosity. It is undoubtedly in a woman's interest to be more desired or else she would turn into a common, unexciting sight.

Man's right to divorce is countered on the other side by a similar right for the woman. She can sue for divorce and get it if she advances sufficient justifications. A woman can lay down a condition in the marriage contract reserving to her the right of divorce without a court case; in this way she would have the same right to divorce as that of the man.

Islam gives certain rights to the muslim wife that wives in Europe, for example, have not attained. She **receives** a **Mahr** (obligatory marriage endowment) whereas in Europe she **pays** a dowry. She has the right to manage her possessions as she pleases whereas European wives lose that right as soon as they marry with the husband becoming the guardian over their property.

Beating and desertion of the marriage bed are forms of treatment reserved only for the disobedient or rebellious wife. A man is obliged to treat his 'normal' wife with all kindness and love. As a matter of fact, those forms of treatment reveal the Quran's amazing insight into the phenomenon of wife-disobedience or rebelliousness (**Noshooz**) and they also accord with the latest findings of modern psychology about the abnormal behaviour of women. We know that psychology divides abnormal behaviour into two kinds. The first is that form of submissiveness scientifically known as 'masochism' – the abnormal condition in which a woman finds pleasure in being beaten, tormented, and subjugated. The other kind is the domineering behaviour or 'sadism', to put it in psychological jargon. It is that abnormal condition in which a woman derives pleasure from domineering, controlling, subjecting, tyrannizing over, and inflicting harm on others. The only way to deal with such a type is to disarm her and render her weapon of hegemony useless. That weapon is her femininity and by deserting her bed she is disarmed. As for the first abnormal type, the woman who finds pleasure only in being beaten and subjected, beating will be the best cure for her.

It is from such analysis that we can grasp the implications of the Quranic verse:

> "As for those from whom you fear disobedience, admonish them and **send them to beds apart and beat them.** Then if they obey you, take no further action against them."
>
> **Women,** 34.

In just a few words – the underlined – we find a miraculously scientific summary of whole volumes containing psychology's studies of female rebelliousness and its treatment.

We turn next to what my friend called the issue of "slavegirls you may own" which brings us to Islam's position on slavery and the Orientalists' accusation that it encouraged that form of injustice. The truth is that Islam never promoted slavery but was the only religion to call for its liquidation. If we read the Bible and St. Paul's Epistle to the Ephesians we will find the following in the latter document:

> "Slaves: obey your masters with such fear and trembling in your heart as you have for God."

The Bible did not enjoin liquidating slavery as a social system; the utmost it called for was to command love and humane treatment between the slaves and their masters.

In the Torah that is in our hands today a treatment even worse than that of slaves was envisaged for freemen. It commanded that if a town surrendered without a fight its people should be taken as captives and slaves. On the other hand, the town which puts up resistance and then capitulates is to receive a far more terrible chastisement. Its old men, youths, women, and children will be massacred.

Slavery, then was an established practice before the revelation of Islam. Preceding religions recommended the slave's loyalty to the master. The Quran came to be the first heavenly revelation to speak about 'freeing necks' and about their emancipation.

The Quran did not clearly and openly prohibit slavery; neither did it command the dismissal of existing slaves. For a sudden dismissal by a Quranic injunction of what amounted at that time to hundreds of thousands of slaves without giving them jobs or any form of social functions would have meant a real social catastrophe. It would have created hundreds of thousands of beggars accosting people in the streets asking for sustenance or being forced to resort to theft and prostitution for a living. This is, certainly, a fate worse than slavery.

The Quranic solution for such dilemma was to stop the taking of slaves and then to work to free the existing numbers. The source of slavery at that time was the enslavement of prisoners of war. Hence, the Quran stipulated that captives be set free or ransomed and not to be taken in slavery: 'Then grant them freedom or take ransom from them', (Muhammad, 4). This means that a prisoner of war is either to be favoured with release for God's sake or ransomed.

As for the already existing slaves, they – in the Quranic

plan – would be gradually emancipated by making the release or freeing of a 'neck' (a slave) an expiation for a number of transgressions both great and slight. In this way, slavery was planned to be liquidated in stages.

It is reasonable, however, to enquire about the sort of treatment meted by masters to their slave-girls before the envisaged end of slavery is attained. This is the topic that so perplexed my friend. The answer is simple: Islam permitted the master to live with any slave-girl **as his wife**. There is no doubt that living with the woman-slave as a wife was, at that time, an honourable and not a degrading treatment.

Above all, Islam's attitude to the slave, making him or her a brother or sister in faith and not a mere down-trodden serf, should not be forgotten:

> "The believers are a band of brothers."
> **The Chambers,** 10

> "It was He who created you from a single soul."
> **The Heights,** 189

> "None of us shall set up mortals as gods besides Him."
> **The Imrans,** 64

Muhammad, peace be upon him, gave the example when he adopted a slave, Zeid Ibn Haretha, emancipating him and even marrying him to Zeinab Bent Gahsh, the free woman and descendant of a noble house. All this was designed to deal a blow at arrogance and bigotry and to set a precedent in the emancipation of slaves that can be followed by others. The Prophet wanted to make it clear, in deed and example, that his mission is to free the slaves.

We come, finally, to man's authority over woman. This is fact of life whether in Islamic, Christian, or godless countries. In atheist Moscow, the rulers have been men from the days of Lenin, Stalin, Khrushchev, and Bolganin to our own time. In France, England (written, of course, before Mrs. Thatcher became prime minister), or any place on earth you care to name it is men who govern, legislate, and invent. All prophets and philosophers have been men. Even music composers have been mostly men although composition is an imaginative activity that does not require 'male muscles'. As the Egyptian thinker El-'Akkad said sarcastically: 'Men have even excelled in and then completely dominated such "feminine specialities" as cooking, sewing, and dress-making'.

Islamic Shari'a has not contributed to the creation of such phenomena as the above which exist in those parts of the world where no Shari'a or Quran have sway. We are simply dealing with facts: men have authority or transcendence over women by virtue of their natural attributes, fitness, and the controlling personality given to them by the Creator. If, here and there, a woman minister, leader, or ruler appears, she is the exception that confirms the rule and the way in which she is much talked about proves the abnormality of the event.

Islam, in fact, did no more than recognize this human rule. This explains why the Quran allotted man double the woman's share in inheritance: because it is man who spends on the family and who works to support it.

Islam's position on women is justice itself. The Prophet's conduct with his wives was the epitome of love, kindness, and tenderness. Wasn't he quoted as saying:

"Of your world women and perfume were made dear to me; and my heart's content is in prayer."

He mentioned women with fragrance, perfume, and prayers which is a very high rank of cherishing indeed. The last thing he said in the last speech before his death was a famous recommendation for the well-being of and respect for women.

If God has elected woman for home and man for the street, it is because He assigned to the latter the trust of building and construction in the earth while He entrusted women with a far greater mission which is the bringing up of humanity itself. It is far more elevating to woman's status to be given such trust.

Can it, then, be rightly alleged that Islam has wronged women?

VIII

The Spirit

My learned friend had the air of someone who knew that he was posing a problem very difficult to discuss. He started to question me:

– What evidence can you give to prove that man has a spirit, that he will be resurrected after death, and that he is not just that body that ends in eust? What does religion say, for example, about spirit¿summoning in sỳ¡ances?

– After a few moments of thinking I began to take the challenge:

Your question today is undouzteely very difficult. Discussing the spirit is like wandering in a labyrinth; there are very few facts known about this subject and yet the little there is supports our own position not yours.

I fell silent for a minute of deep thinking and then resumed my answer to him:

Please, follow my line of thinking. The first indication which aids us in finding evidence for the existence of the spirit is that man has a double nature.

Man has two natures. There is firstly an external, apparent, visible nature which is his body. This has all the attributes of matter. It can be weighed and measured; it occupies a portion of space and time; it is continually changing, moving, and 'becoming' from one condition to the other and from one moment to the next. The body is subject to all conditions of health, sickness, fatness, leanness, ruddiness, paleness, vitality, satiety, etc. Appended to the physical nature we find a continuous 'tape' of sensations, emotions, instincts, and fears which never, even for one instant, stops unwinding in the brain.

In so far as this primary nature and the sensations appended to it have the characteristics of matter, we can say that man's body and his 'animal spirit' belong to matter.

There is, however, another nature inside man which is totally different from the first in quality. It is characterized by fixity and permanence; it is above time and space. This nature is what we call 'reason' with its unchanging standards, axioms, and deductions. It is also the conscience with its judgments and the aesthetic sense. It is summed up in the ego which consists of all the previous faculties: mind, conscience, aesthetic and ethical sense. The ego is completely other than the body and the 'animal spirit' or instincts which can be enflamed with hunger and desire.

The ego is the absolute, fundamental identity through which man experiences that profound sense of presence, being, presentation to, and attendance in the world. He feels that he is and has always been **here.** This is a fixed, unchanging, and continuous sense which does not wax or wane or grows ill or ages with time. It knows no past, present, or future; but is an enduring present or 'now' that does not elapse as sensations fade into the past. Its essence is that awareness of duration and permanence.

It is here that we encounter another kind of existence

which transcends the attributes of matter: it does not change, it does not occupy a position in space-time, and it cannot be weighed and measured. On the contrary, this form of existence is the constant by which variables are measured; it is the absolute by which we come to know all that is relative in the dimension of matter.

The most accurate description of this type of existence is that it is spiritual in nature.

We may go on to ask: which of the two natures constitute man in reality? Is 'true' man the body or the spirit? To know the answer we have to establish which of the two natures governs the other.

The materialists claim that man is just his body which is the controlling nature. All the elements I have been enumerating – reason, aesthetic and ethical sense, conscience, and that 'superstition' we call identity or the ego – they deem mere secondary effects of the body, manipulated by it and serving and satisfying its lusts and passions.

This materialistic concept is erroneous. The truth is that the body is servant not master, compliant and not imperious. Doesn't the body feel hunger but we refuse to oblige it with food because we have previously decided to fast that particular day in worship of God? Isn't it aroused with lust but we restrain it?

Doesn't our body begin spontaneously from the moment we wake up in the morning to carry out 'a plan of action' formulated to the smallest detail by the mind? Who is leader here and who is led?

Where is the body's dominance at the moment of self-immolation when a commando, for example, ties an explosive belt round his waist and marches forward to zlow up a tank with the enemy soldiers inside it? What bodily interest does he serve zy his death? Which nature controls the other here? The spirit resolves to destroy the body in a purely idealistic moment which no materialistic doctrine can explain away by reference to any tangible gains. The body cannot resist such resolve; it has no power to counter it and has no option but to fade away completely. It is here that we know which of the two existences is the more ascendant, which of them really constitutes the essence of man.

We possess nowadays more than one proof that the body is the secondary form of existence: all operations of amputation, substitution, or transplanting of body parts; reports of 'electric' hearts, artificial kindeys, blood and cornea banks; and those 'stores of human accessories' where legs, arms, and hearts can be replaced or fitted on.

It would not be an unbelievable joke to hear that a bridegroom may surprise his bride in the year 2000 to find her taking off her whig, dentures, foam-ruzber breasts, artificial eye, and wooden leg leaving nothing behind but a 'chassis' like that of a car where the seats, doors, and upholstery have been removed.

The body undergoes extensive replacements without the character being correspondingly affected because the substituted arm or leg or eye or breast is not what contributes to make up man. Thus, they are removed and replaced even zy batteries, metal rods, or pieces of aluminium and nothing happens to 'man' because he is not merely the sum of these members but is the spirit which presides at 'the driving wheel' and controls that machine we call the body.

The spirit is not the brain zut the managing agent of the body and it is represented by a 'board of directors' working out of the brain's cells. The brain, just as the body's cells, complies with the orders issued to it and reveals them in its actions; in the end, however, it is only a 'glove' worn by that invisible hand, the spirit, to act with it in the material world.

All this evidence leads us to grasp that man has two natures: an essential, ruling nature which is his spirit and a secondary, transient one; namely, his body. What occurs in death is that the second nature passes away while the immortal spirit joins eternity. The body goes to dust but the spirit ascends to its immortal world.

To those who prefer philosophical arguments we can produce yet another proof of the spirit's existence. This proof is drawn from the peculiarities of motion. For motion can only be observed from a point outside it; you cannot perceive the motion of which you are a part but you must have an external point from which you can observe it. This explains why you may not at certain moments be azle to know whether the lift you are in has stopped moving or not because you have become an integral part of its movement. You can only perceive the lift's movements if you look through its door to the fixed platforms outside. The same applies to a train speeding on its rails. You can perceive its speed, while you are inside it, only at the moment it stops or if you look out of the window at some fixed landmarks. Similarly, the sun's movement cannot be observed by a person standing on its surface, if that is possible, but it can be observed from the earth or the moon. In like manner, the earth's movement can ze observed from the moon and not from its own surface.

The principle is that you cannot fully perceive a thing or state unless you are outside it. Thus, we could not possibly have been able to perceive the passage of time if the perceiving part in us has not been implanted in a separate 'threshold' external to that continual passage; that is, in a 'threshold of eternity'. If our perception of time moved with every jump of the seconds hand of our clocks, we would not have ever perceived the passage of those seconds and our perception of them would have just faded away as they elapse without leaving a trace.

This is a stunning conclusion to draw and it means that part of our being iis external to the framework of the temporal contiuum. It is immortal, it can observe time from a point of stillness and perceive it without being implicated in it. It, therefore, neither ages nor elapses. When the body crumbles into dust, that part will remain as it is to live its own, non-temporal life – that part is the spirit.

Each one of us can sense that spiritual existence deep down as a state of presence, permanence, attendance, and being which is totally unlike that material existence with its changes, fluctuations, and pulses which occur with the passage of time outside it. This internal state I call 'presence', and of which we are conscious at moments of inner awareness, is the key to our spiritual existence and to that puzzle – the spirit.

Another evidence to our spiritual nature is our intuitive sense of freedom. If we were mere material bodies governed within the framework of material existence by inevitable material laws, this intuitive sense of freedom would be inconceivable.

We have, then, a spirit that transcends time, death, and the material inevitabilities. But what about resurrection? No one has so far returned from the kingdom of death to tell us what experiences he underwent. The Day of Resurrection has not yet arrived for us to point to a tangible, incontrovertible proof. All that can be said about resurrection is that it is a religious fact which both reason and science find probable. But why should these two latter find it probable?

All the phenomena and aspects of the universe indicate that everything passes through a complete circle where the end is followed by a new beginning: night comes after day and then the day dawns again; the sun rises and sets to rise once more. The four seasons follow each other in a repeated cycle. Such observations make the waking involved in resurrection probable after the sleep of death; for everything returns to where it began or is renewed. God refers to himself in the Quran as the Originator and Restorer:

> "You shall return to Him as He created you."
>
> **The Heights,** 29

> "He gives being to all His creatures, and in the end He will bring them zack to life;"
>
> **Jonah,** 4

Isn't it observed that everything moves in orbits from atoms to galaxies? Even civilizations and history have cycles. This eternal renewal favours the possibility of resurrection.

Another proof we may cite in favour of the truth of resurrection is the order, accurate to precision, which governs the universe from the largest galaxy down to the smallest atom without the slightest sign of aberration. Even the invisible sub-atomic electron is governed by that order and law. This infinetisimal part cannot move from one orbit to another within the same atom unless it discharges or absorbs an amount of energy equalling that taken by its jump. It is more like a train traveller who cannot go anywhere without a ticket.

Given this very tightly-woven order how can we imagine that a murderer or an unjust person can escape retribution simply because he has managed to elude the police. The mind finds it justifiable to conceive that this person will necessarily be punished and that there must be another life in which scores are settled – this is what justice decrees.

We are zorn to love, to seek, and to strive for the achievement of justice. Nevertheless, justice is absent from our world. If some thinkers consider that thirst for water proves the existence of water, we can, similarly, contend that longing for justice is evidence that justice exists if not in our world then, zy necessity, at a future time and hour when its scales will be erected.

All the previous hints are indications that point to and favour the reality of resurrection, reckoning, and the next life. A person who believes in the Quran, however, has no need for such proofs because his heart has reached certainty thus relieving him from arguing.

It remains for us to ask what is the spirit?
The Quran says:
> "They ask you about the Sprity. Say:
> 'The Spirit is of my Lord's Knowledge.
> Little indeed is the Knowledge
> Vouchsafed to you".
> **The Night Journey,** 85

The Spirit is a puzzle about which no one knows anything. It is striking that whenever the Spirit is mentioned in the Quran the words 'of my Lord's knowledge' or 'command' or others of similar meaning, accompany it:

> "He lets the Spirit (by His command) descend on those of His servants whom He chooses."
> **The Forgiver, 15**

> "By His will he sends down the angels with the Spirit to those of his servants whom He chooses,"
> **The Bee, 2**

> "On that night the angels and the Spirit by their Lord's leave come down with His decrees."
> **Qadr, 4**

> "Thus we have inspired you with a Spirit of Our will."
> **Counsel, 52**

We always encounter the same words whenever 'spirit' is mentioned: 'Our will', 'of my Lord's knowledge', 'by his leave'. Can God's Will be a spirit? Or can His Word be a Spirit? Didn't He speak about Jesus, peace on him, in the following words:

> "A word from Him. His name is Messiah, Jesus the son of Mary."
> **The Imrans, 45**

God also said that Jesus is 'His word which he cast to Mary; a Spirit form Him'. **Woman, 171**

I come finally to my friend's query about 'the summoning of spirits'. This phenomenon is suspect in the eyes of believers. They doubt that what occurs in the darkened rooms of séances is caused by the presence of this or that spirit. A prominent thinker like Henri Soder, for instance, says that such phenomena originate in the medium's subconscious and through his or her psychic powers; according to him, nothing in fact, is summoned

Some Indian thinkers believe that what really enters the medium's body during the séance are some nether world spirits which know certain facts about the dead and use them to ridicule those present and have fun at their expense.

Muslim sufis, for their part, say that it is not the spirit which attends the séances but its **Kareen** or Double; that is the jinni who accompanied the dead person during his life. The jinni knows all the dead man's secrets by virtue of such 'company'. As the jinn live much longer than man, the Double survives his human mate and it is he who attends séances divulging the secrets of his mate and imitating his voice and manners to poke fun at those present in accordance with the jinn's hostility towards human beings.

Those sufis resort to a vivid illustration of their view. They say that if we ring the bell in an office the servant will show up to enquire about our requests but the master or director of the office will not leave his domain so easily to attend on us. The same, they add, applies to the world of spirits. It is nether spirits, the jinn and such like who are summoned in séances and who impose on their audiences.

The human spirits abide in another world; namely, the **Barzakh** or Barrier. They cannot be recalled but they may communicate with whomever they wish either in dreams or, indeed, in wakefulness provided the appropriate conditions exist.

On the evidence of the many séances I attended and the particular experiences I had of that sphere I can say that there is no proof that the phenomena of the séance room are due to the presence of the intended spirits.

The view of the muslim sufis may be the nearest explanation to the truth of such occurrences. The matter is still open for study. It is regrettable, however, that superstitions are far in excess of the facts in this area. The last word has not been uttered yet.

You, my friend, will undoubtedly laugh at hearing such words as the jinn, the nether spirits, or the Double. You will be quite right there. If you do not believe that you have a soul, how can you be expected to believe in a jinni; if you do not believe in God how can it be possible for you to believe in the existence of the devils?

Yet, if you have been born a hundred years ago and someone came to you with a talk about an invisible ray that goes through iron, or about pictures that travel the air across the oceans in less than a second, or about a man who walks over the dusty surface of the moon wouldn't you have laughed and chuckled at what he says many times more than your laughter in ridicule of what I now say to you? You would have accused him of being a fugitive from a mental asylum. His predictions, however, are now facts that are all too apparent before our eyes and ears.

IX

The Conscience

'You speak reverently about conscience', said my friend, 'as if it were an absolute entity. It is, however, a social product. It is no more than a copper currency minted and stamped in the forge of social dealings. In my opinion, its judgments and criteria change according to the dominant and current interests. That value which brings benefit I describe as good, that which harms I label bad even if it were chastity which you hold as dear as your eyes.'

I started to reply calmly:

Yes, I believe that this is the view of the materialistic philosophy, at least according to what I hear. It sees in conscience a deterrent and admonitory authority that sprang out of social factors; it is just the outcome of a certain experience that varies from one person to another and from one age to the other.

The truth, however, gives you the lie, my friend. The truth is that conscience is a light implanted by God in the human constitution. It is an inborn indicator, guide, or compass directing us to the truths of life. All that social cultivation has to do in this regard is to polish and refine that instrument.

We have evidence to support our view and refute yours. Consider the animal kingdom where no 'society' exists. You find the cat defecating and then turning to cover its faeces with dust. From what 'feline society' did it catch this habit? How was it able to distinguish between filth and cleanliness? Likewise, if you catch a cat stealing fish and hit it on the head, it would bend it down fixing its eyes on the ground in a manifest sense of guilt. If the same cat happens to break a vase while playing with the children in the house, it would hurriedly run to hide in fear under a chair realizing that it had done something wrong.

All these are signs and indicators of conscience. Feline community does not necessitate the emergence of such feelings. That community itself does not even exist.

Consider also 'marital' fidelity in doves, the horse's noble attachmnt to its owner till death, the lion's proud mein and its refusal to attack its prey from behind, the camel's shyness that impels it to stop sexual intercourse with the female if it sensed an observer. Moreover, I remind you of that serious incident seen by the spectators at the National Circus in Cairo years ago. The lion jumped at its trainer, Muhammad Helou, from behind setting its claws in his shoulders and mortally wounding him. Circus officials report that the lion subsequently refused to eat or to leave his cage. It was transferred to the zoo and given a female to entertain it but it attacked its companion and forced it out. It continued to refuse food and, finally, kept biting its guilty hand till it bled to death.

Here we encounter an animal that takes its own life in grief and atonement for its crime. From what 'society' in the world of lions did it adopt this attitude? Do lion communities hold the devouring of man a crime deserving suicide as a punishment?

We confront in this situation a kind of nobility, morality, or conscientious behaviour that we can hardly find in a human. We are, in fact, witnessing the total collapse of the materialistic conception and interpretation of the nature of conscience.

There can be no explanation for what we see except that presented by religion; namely, that conscience is a light implanted by God in human nature and that the entire social role in this connection is to remove the 'rust' covering the soul and allow it to reveal that divine light. This is actually what occurred in the incident between the lion and its trainer. The joint life, love, and companionship polished that animal's self awakening the divine spark and making the lion experience sadness and repentance and then kill itself in sorrow like the humans.

Our Prophet, peace be upon him, said: 'That which is lawful is clear and that which is probibited is clear.' He also said, 'Consult your heart even if you have been advised by man.' We are in no need of a 'Faculty of Shari'a Studies' to know right from wrong, truth from falsehood, lawful from unlawful. God has placed in the heart of each of us a Shari'a Faculty and a scale that cannot go wrong. All that is required of us is to purify ourselves of the dross of matter and the pressure of desires so that we can 'see', 'know', and 'distinguish' without leaning on the crotchet of 'social experience' but with the aid of God's light – the conscience:

> "Believers, if you fear God, He will
> give you guidance"
>
> **The Spoils,** 29

God inspired the mystic Muhammad Ibn Abdel-Gabbar with the phrase: "How can you despair of Me while in your heart is My envoy and speaker."

The conscience is an eternal truth. The basic ethical values are similarly fixed. Killing an innocent person will never become a virtue, nor will theft, lying, harming others, vice, lechery, harshness, scurrility, cruelty, hypocrisy, or treachery. All these are moral defects and they will so remain until God inherits the earth and all that is on it.

Love, mercy, truthfulness, forbearance, forgiveness, and generosity will likewise remain virtues for ever. They will never turn into crimes unless the entire heavens and earth are corrupted and reason is annihilated leaving madness to rule supreme.

X

Is Pilgrimage A Pagan Rite?

My friend's eyes had that gleam which characterizes the look of a person preparing to deal a knock-out. His broad smile revealed his teeth and he rubbed his hands in glee as he talked:

– Don't you observe as I do that your pilgrimage rites are frankly pagan? First of all there is that stone structure you call the Ka'ba to which you cling and then go round. There is also the stoning of the devil, the hurrying between Safa and Marwa, the kissing of the Black Stone, and the occurrence of the number seven in many acts such as circling the Ka'ba, stoning the devil, or hurrying to and fro between Safa and Marwa. This is, surely, a vestige of ancient superstitions about talismanic numbers. There is yet that Ihram cloth you wrap round your naked zodies in preparation for the pilgrimage. Don't be angry with me if my frankness hurts you; but, as you say, there is no timidity in the pursuit of knowledge.

Having finished, he started puffing the smoke of his cigarette slowly and fixed his eyes on me from behind his glasses.

I began to reply with equal calm:

Don't **you** observe with me that according to the laws of matter we studied it is found that the smaller body revolves round the larger: the electron in the atom circles round the nucleus, the moon round the earth, the earth round the sun, the sun round the galaxy, the galaxy round a bigger one, and so on till we ascend to the Absolute Greatest: God? Don't we repeat the phrase 'Allah is greater' (**Allahu Akzar**) meaning that He is bigger than everything? Hence, and in accordance with the laws of your science, everything should revolve round Him. **You** are now, in fact, revolving round Him in spite of yourself along with our solar system. You cannot choose but revolve for nothing is still in the universe but God – the Sanctuary, the Enduring; He is still whereas everything else is in movement around him.

So far for the law of the lesser and the greater which you studied in physics. As for us, we circle around God's House of our own free will. This House, the Ka'ba, was the first building man devoted to the worship of God. Ever since that time immemorial it has become a symbol and a House of God. Don't you 'circle' the Kremlin revering a certain man entombed there and claiming that he saved mankind. If you know where Shakespeare is zuried, you would race each other to visit his grave in more fervour than we have as we vie for the journey to the tomb of Muhammad, peace be upon him. Don't you lay a wreath on a stone monument saying that it is a symbol of the unknown soldier? Why, then, blame us for casting a stone at a certain post which we take to symbolize Satan? Don't you live in a ceaseless 'hurrying' from the moment of your birth to that of your death and doesn't your son, after your death, repeat that 'hurrying' all over again? This is the same as the symbolic 'hurrying' from Safa – the name in Arabic connotes emptiness or vacuum as a symbol of nothingness – to Marwa, the spring which signifies life and being. Isn't this, in fact, the pendulous movement of all creatures? Can't you discern in the rites of pilgrimage a profound symbolic synopsis of all these mysteries?

Now for the number seven that moves you to so much sarcasm. Let me ask you, in my turn, why do we have seven tones in the musical scale: Sol, La, C, Do, Re, Mi, Fa? After the seventh tone we return again to the pitch of Sol – always seven tones and not eight or more. The shades of the light spectrum are seven, electrons revolve round the nucleus in seven fields, the embryo completes its growth only in the seventh month and if delivered before that time will be stillborn. The days of the week are seven – among all peoples – and this was reached without any previous agreement. Doesn't all this signify something? Or is it that all these facts are, for their part, mere talismanic superstitions?

Let me further ask you: don't you kiss a letter your beloved sent you? Are you, then, a pagan? Why blame us, therefore, for kissing that Black Stone which our Prophet Muhammad, peace be upon him, carried in his own robe and kissed? There is no paganism involved at all; for we do not address our devotion and worship to the stones but to the profound meanings, symbols, and memories they evoke.

The pilgrimage actions are occasions for inducing contemplation, arousing the feelings, and instilling godliness in the heart. The Ihram cloth we wrap round our naked bodies, and which should not be sewn, symbolizes the renunciation of worldly ornament and complete devotion before the Presence of the Creator. It is just the same as our condition at birth and death; for we come to the world wrapped in a piece of cloth and go out of it in the same attire. Don't you need formal suits for audiences with kings? We, for our part, say that only such stripping of ornament and donning of this simple robe is appropriate for God's Majesty; for He is greater than all kings and nothing more befits attendance before Him than absolute humility and the shedding of clothes. The humble Ihram robe worn in God's Presence by rich and poor, Raj and millionaire alike signifies also that men are zrothers however different they may be in ranks and wealth.

For us the pilgrimage is a great gathering, an annual conference; it is an enlarged version, if you like, of the Friday prayers – that smaller meeting which unites us every week. These events have wonderful significance for anyone who cares to contemplate their meanings. They are as far removed from paganism as can be imagined.

If you had stood, as I did, on Mount Arafat, one among millions crying 'Allahu Akbar', reciting the Quran in more than twenty tongues, calling out **'labbayka Allahuma labbayk'** (we have answered your call, God), sobbing, and melting in love and longing – you would have shed tears unconsciously and merged in that multitude of men, you would have experienced that sense of reverence and annihilation of self before God, the Magnificent, the Lord of all Being, Who masters everything there is.

XI

Could Muhammad Be The Author of The Quran?

My friend spoke slowly choosing his words:

– I don't really want to hurt you, for I know how much you cherish the Quran. I concur with you that it is a worthy book. But why couldn't it have been compiled by Muhammad himself? It wouldn't be out of the ordinary if a man as great as he was should write a book as valuable as the Quran. This, certainly, would be a more logical explanation than the claim that the Quran was revealed by God. We have never observed God in the process of sending anythins down from heaven. We live in an age in which it is difficult to persuade anyone that an angel called Gabriel came down from heaven with a book to reveal it to a certain person.

I replied in my usual quiet voice:

– On the contrary, we live in an age in which it is completely easy to believe that there are invisible angels and that truths can come to men in inspiration. Our moderns speak nowadays of flying saucers that come from distant planets to land on earth, of invisible rays that can kill, of radio waves that home on to targets to facilitate their destruction, of pictures that are transformed into frequencies in the air and then materialize again as they are received in sets as small as cigarette packets, of cameras that take pictures of 'ghosts', of eyes that see in the dark, of a man who walked on the moon.

It is no longer an inconceivable thing to hear that God has sent an invisible angel to deliver His revelation to one of his prophets. Gabriel's existence has, in fact, become a stale fact in our age; it is less strange and amazing than many things we see or hear about every day.

You ask, 'Why shouldn't we say that the Quran has been composed by Muhammad (peace be upon him)?' The reply is that we cannot do this. With its form, phrases, and even letters, and with the knowledge, science, mysteries, stylistic beauty, and linguistic precision it contains, it is impossible to conceive that any man is capable of composing it. Add to this the fact that Muhammad, peace be upon him, was illiterate; he could not read or write, he did not attend any school, and he did not travel outside the Arabian Peninsula or get acquainted with any civilization. To doubt the source of the Quran, or even just to enquire about it as you do, is indeed impossible in the light of what I have just said. God, in fact, challenges disbelievers like you who alleged, in the Prophet's time, that the Quran is of human authorship:

> "Say: 'Then bring a sura like it, and call (for help) on all you can besides God, if you are truthful."
>
> **Jonah,** 38.

God is daring them to enlist the help of the jinn, the angels, and the geniuses among men to compose even one verse similar to those of the Quran. That challenge is still standing and no one has yet come up with anything in answer.

Indeed, if we study the Quran in fairness and objectivity, we will completely rule out that Muhammad, peace be upon him, was its author. If, first of all, he had really been its author, he would have voiced his cares and grief in it. In one and the same year, his wife, Khadeeja, and his paternal uncle, Abu Taleb, died. They were his only supports in life and the loss he sustained in their departure was incalculable. Yet no word is mentioned in the Quran about them. The Quran also remains silent about the death of Ibrahim, Muhammad's only son over whom he grieved. The Quran is, in fact, totally separate from Muhammad's self.

Sometimes a Quranic verse would come to contradict what Muhammad has been doing or thinking. At other times, a verse would be revealed to adomnish him, as when he turned to the nobles of Quraysh leaving the blind man who came to listen to him:

> "He frowned and turned his back when the blind man came towards him. How could you tell, he might have sought to purify himself. He might have been forewarned, and might have profited from Our warning."
>
> **He Frowned, 1–4**

A verse would come at times to revoke a measure of the Prophet's:

> "A prophet may not take captives until he has fought and made slaughter in the land. You (the Prophet's followers) seek the chance gain of this world, but God desires for you the world to come. He is mighty and wise. Had there not been a previous

> sanction from God, you would have been sternly punished for that which you have taken."
>
> **The Spoils,** 67–8

Sometimes the Quran commands Muhammad, peace be upon him, to communicate to his followers that which he could not have possibly said if he had been the author of the Quran:

> "Say: 'I am no prodigy among the prophets; nor do I know what will be done with me or you."
>
> **Al-Ahqaf,** 9

No prophet can, of his own accord, inform his followers that he does not know what will happen to him and to them or that he cannot bring benefit or ward off harm either with regard to himself or to them. They would desert him, if he did so. In fact, the jews took advantage of the above verse to justify their charge that our Prophet was really a useless man for he did not know what will be done to himself or to his followers. If the Prophet had been the author of the Quran, such verses could not have been found in that book.

Secondly, if we examine the style of the Quranic phrase, we will find that it is completely new and unique in its syntax or structure. It is quite different from anything that came before or since in Arabic literature. We can almost go to the extent of dividing everything extant in Arabic into poetry, prose, and Quran. This latter is a kind apart neither poetic nor prosaic. For rhythm in poetry is the outcome of meter and rhyme. This is seen, for example, in a line of poetry by Ibn el-Abbas al-Asadi:

> Akfara men ahlihi 'Obayd
> (Obeid has lost all his kinsmen)
> Falaysa yobdi wala yo'eed.
> (He can no longer initiate or settle matters).

The rhythm in this line derives from its division into two hemistiches rhyming together with a long 'd' sound. It is, in fact, what is called 'externally induced rhythm'. The Quran's rhythm or music, on the other hand, is internal:

> "Wad-dhoha, wal-layli etha saga"
> (By the morning hours, and by the night when most still)
>
> **The Morning Hours, 1**

There are no hemistiches or rhyme in this straight forward phrase, but it is redolent with rhythm. From whence did such rhythm come? It is internal music.

Listen to the following verses:

> "My Lord! Lo! My bones wax feeble and my head is shining with grey hair. Yet, never, Lord, have I prayed to you in vain."
>
> **Mary, 4**

> "Taha. We have not revealed unto you (Muhammad) the Quran that you should be distressed. But as a reminder unto him who fears. A Revelation from him who created the earth and the high heavens. The Beneficent One, Who is established on the Throne"
>
> **Taha. 1–4**

If the topic dealt with is a threat the sentence structure and morphology become like chunks of flint stone and its rhythm produces a sort of metallic screeching that pierces the ears:

> "On a day of unremitting woe we let loose on them a howling wind which snatched them off as if they had been trunks of uprooted palm-trees."
>
> **The Moon,** 19–20

Words like 'howling' and 'uprooted' strike our ears with their sounds in Arabic, like pieces of rock.

If Quranic verses report a major event, like those that speak about the end of the Flood, their sentences become very short as if they were Morse Code signals. A verse in its entirety becomes like a pithy telegram with a momentous impact:

> "A voice cried out: 'Earth swallow up your waters; heaven, cease your rain! The floods abated and God's will was done."
>
> **Houd,** 44

Such varying effects in word morphology, syntax, and the concordance of rhythms with meanings and feelings reach to the very summit in the Quran. They are always achieved in a smooth and easy manner without any artificiality or affectation.

Thirdly, if we further pursue this line of analysis, we will discover a meticulous accuracy and staggering adequacy: every letter is in its precise place neither advanced nor retarded. You cannot substitute one word for another, nor put one letter in place of the other. Every word has been chosen from among millions by a very sensitive act of discernment.

We shall presently encounter such accuracy as has never been equalled in composition. Examine, for example, the word 'fertilizing' in the following verse:

> "We let loose the fertilizing wind"
>
> **Al-Hijr,** 22

It was in the past understood in a figurative sense to mean that the wind stimulates the clouds causing them to rain; the rain would then 'fertilize' the soil, that is, make it productive. Nowadays, however, we know that the winds drive positively-charged clouds into negatively-charged ones causing lightning, thunder, and rain. In this sense they 'fertilize' the clouds. We also know that winds carry the pollen from one flower to the other thus literally fertilizing them. Hence, we are before a word which is true figuratively, literally, and scientifically. It is, moreover, aesthetically superb and rhythmically pleasing. This is what we mean by meticulous accuracy in the choice and placing of a word.

Let us also consider the following verse:

> "Do not usurp each other's property by unjust means, nor bribe judges with it in order that you may knowingly and wrongfully deprive others of their possessions."
>
> **The Cow,** 188

The Arabic word used for 'bribe' here is **'todloo'** which literally means to 'lower' something or send it down. This may seem a strange use putting in mind that the judge or ruler to whom the money is given is in a higher not a lower position vis-à-vis the givers. The Quran, however, effects an appropriate correction with this use: the hand that accepts zribes **is a lower** hand even if it is the ruler's or the judge's. This is how the expression 'lower it down to the judges' comes in an unequalled stylistic adequacy to convey the meanness and degradation of those who receive bribes.

In a verse about jihad or holy struggle we read:

> "O, Believers, why is it that when it is said to you: 'March in the cause of God', you are bowed down to the ground with heaviness."
>
> **Repentance,** 38

The Quran uses the elided from – **Iththakaltum** – of the verb **tathakaltum** ('bowed down to the ground with heaviness') to vividly express the cowardice of some who cling and stick to the ground in terror when they are called upon to fight. The elision of the 't' sound found at the beginning of the original form of the verb and its merger into the 'th' sound eloquently conveys the sticking of the cowards to the ground for dear life.

The Quran speaks about the killing of children for fear of poverty in two similar verses which only differ in a significant respect:

> "You shall not kill your children because you cannot support them. We provide **for you and for them:**"
>
> **Cattle.** 151

> "You shall not kill your children for fear of want. We will provide **for them and for you.**"
>
> **The Night Journey,** 31

The underlined difference in word order is not haphazard but calculated. When the killing of children is motivated by actual want, by the poverty of the family **at that time**, the Quranic emphasis is on God's succour of the parents; hence, they are mentioned first (in the first verse). If, on the other hand, the killing is impelled zy fear of expected want, of the future possibility of poverty, the Quran delivers its assuring message by placing the children (the future) before the family as recipients of God's provision (in the second verse). Such minutiae can hardly occur to the mind of any **human** author.

Similar cases in the Quran of advancing or retarding words are always meaningful. In the verse which lays down the punishment for theft the male thief is mentioned before the female whereas in that which speaks about fornication the fornicatress is mentioned before the fornicator. The reason behind such ordering is quite obvious: in cases of theft man is always more daring and the initiator, but in fornication it is usually the woman who initiates the train of events; she lays the snares for the intended man from the very moment she stands zefore the mirror making her face up, wearing her perfume, or selecting a short dress. Thus, the Quran:

> "The adulteress and the adulterer, scourge you each of them a hundred lashes."
>
> **Light,** 2

> "As for the thief both male and female, cut off their hands in punishment for their deeds."
> **The Table, 38**

In more than sixteen places in the Quran, 'hearing' is mentioned before 'sight' when zoth come together:

> "and gave you ears and eyes and hearts; so that you may give thanks."
> **The Bee, 78**

> "and gave them ears and eyes and hearts."
> **Al-Ahquf, 26**

> "Hear and see them on the Day they come unto Us."
> **Mary, 38**

> "The hearing, sight, and heart of man shall be questioned."
> **The Night Journey, 36**

> "You did not hide yourselves, so that your ears and eyes and skins could not observe you."
> **Fussilat, 22**

> "He also hears all and sees all"
> **Counsel, 11**

Hearing, as we can see from the previous verses, invariably comes first.

It is unquestionable that the sense of hearing is more sensitive and developed than sight. We hear the jinn but we do not see them. The prophets heard the words of God and spoke with Him but none of them saw Him. Muhammad, peace be upon him, received the Quran through hearing. The mother can distinguish the voice of her child crying even when it is lost in a crowd of people. Hearing in human beings stays active even during sleep when the eyes are resting. Anyone who undertakes an anatomy of the hearing system will find it more sensitive and exact than sight.

The Quran employs a similar technique of word order with regard to wealth and offspring:

> "The day when wealth and children will avail nothing and when none shall be saved except him who comes before his Lord with a pure heart."
> **The Poets, 88**

> "Your wealth and children are but a temptation. God's reward is great."
> **Cheating. 15**

> "Neither their riches nor their children shall in the least protect them from His scourge. They are the heirs of Hell, and there they shall remain for ever."
> **The Imrans, 116**

> "Do they think that in giving them wealth and children we are solicitous for their welfare? By no means! They cannot see."
> **The Believers, 55**

> "Let neither their riches nor their children rouse your desire. Through these God seeks to punish them in this life, so that they shall die unbelievers."
>
> **Repentance, 55**

There are many more verses keeping the same order of mention, the secret behind this is that many people cherish wealth more dearly than their own offspring.

Subtle and exact stylistic touches in the Quran extend to word inflections. In the verse:

> "If two parties of believers take up arms against each other, make peace between them."
>
> **The Chambers, 9**

the two parties are referred to first in the plural mode: the verb **'ektatalo'** – fought among themselves – is used. But later on they are spoken of in the dual mode: in the word **'baynahuma'** which means 'between the two of them'. There is a very subtle and fine touch here. For in the thick of fighting the two parties will merge into each other becoming a 'host' or 'pluralism' of striking arms, zut if at peace they will separate again into two (the dual mode) groups each sending an envoy for talks. Hence the precision of the Quranic manner of expression.

Even propositions and conjunctions are employed in (or are absent from) the Quranic text for weighty considerations and according to a precise and accurate calculation. An example of this method is afforded by a repeated Quranic structure based on the phrase, 'they ask you':

> "They ask you about what they should give in alms. Say: 'What you can spare'."
>
> **The Cow,** 219
>
> "They ask you about the phases of the moon. Say: 'They are timings for people and pilgrimage'."
>
> **The Cow,** 189
>
> "They ask you about the Spirit. Say: 'The Spirit is of my Lord's knowledge'."
>
> **The Night Journey,** 85

The word 'say' **(kol)** comes invariably as an answer to the question introduced by the phrase, 'they ask you'.

An exception, however, occurs when a verse speaks about the condition of the mountains on Doomsday:

> "They ask you about the mountains. Then say: 'My Lord will crush them to fine dust'."
>
> **Ta Ha,** 105

Here the word 'say' comes in Arabic in the form **'fakol'** or 'then say' instead of **'kol'**. The reason is that all previous questions have already been put to Muhammad, but no one has yet asked him about what happens to mountains on Doomsday because this is one of the secrets of that day. Thus, God is in effect saying to him: **if** you are asked about that subject, **THEN SAY** such and such a thing. The prefix **fa** is not superfluous but semantically functional in a calculated manner.

In another verse we read:

> "If My servants ask you about Me, I am near."
>
> **The Cow,** 186

The word 'say' is absent here because the question concerns the essence of God and it is He only who can 'say' anything about that subject.

A similar subtlety is manifest in the Quranic uses of the pronouns 'I' and 'We' in relation to God. For God speaks in the plural 'We' when referring to a divine act in which all His attributes contribute such as creation or the revelation and preservation of the Quran:

> "We revealed the Quran and shall ourselves preserve it."
>
> **Al Hijr,** 9

> "We created you, will you not believe."
>
> **The Event,** 67

> "We revealed the Quran in the night of Kadr."
>
> **Kadr,** 1

> "Behold the semen you discharge: did you create it or We?"
>
> **The Event,** 59

> "We created them and endowed them with strong limbs and joints; but if We please, We can replace them by other men."
>
> **Man,** 28

The pronoun 'We' in these examples expresses the unison of divine attributes as they act in a great original invention such as creation.

If, on the other hand, the verses deal with a situation in which God speaks to a creature of His, as in His talk with Moses, the individual pronoun 'I' is employed:

> "I am God. There is no God zut Me.
> Worship Me, and recite your prayers
> in My remembrance."
>
> **Ta Ha,** 14

God uses 'I' because it is His Essence that is present here and because He wishes to lay stress on His Oneness and on monotheism in worship.

Still pursuing the meticulous accuracy of Quranic expression, we find two identical verses about patience that differ only in an 'l' letter added to a word in the second of them. In the first verse Loqman, the Wise, says to his son:

> "Endure with fortitude whatever
> zefalls you, for this is will-power."
>
> **Loqman,** 17

In the second verse we read:

> "Who endures and forgives this truly
> is will-power."
>
> **Counsel,** 43

Patience in the first verse is "men 'azm el-omoor" (will-power) while in the second it is "Lamen (truly) 'azm el-omoor." The secret behind the emphasis with '**la**' in the latter construction is that the patience involved in this case is doubly more demanding than the endurance exhorted in the first verse. It is patience vis-à-vis an aggression by an opponent and the person advised is required not only to endure but to forgive. This is certainly more difficult than the endurance of unavoidable divine fate.

The same emphatic '**la**' occurs once more to add significance to two similar verses about the sending down of rain and the growth of plants:

> "Consider the water which you drink. Was it you that poured it from the clouds or We? If we please, We could turn it bitter."
> **The Event, 69**

> "Consider the seeds you sow. Is it you that give them growth or We? If We pleased, We could turn your plants into chaff."
> **The Event, 65**

The Arabic word for 'could turn' in the first verse is "**ja' alnahu**" while in the second it is "**laja'alnahu**". The emphatic '**la**' in the latter word is necessitated by the fact that there will certainly ze someone to claim that he can destroy the plants turning them into chaff just as the Creator can. With regard to the former case, however, no human dare allege that he can draw down salt water from the cloues. There is no need for emphasis here.

The same accuracy of expression is found when Ibrahim (Abraham) describes God:

> "Who will cause me to die and bring me back to life hereafter."
> **The Poets,** 81

> "He who gives me food and drink"
> **The Poets,** 79

The word 'He' is brought in the second verse to emphasize divine agency when the provision of food is mentioned because anyone can easily claim that he is the provider of food and drink. No one, however, will claim the ability to cause death and resurrection as God did with Ibrahim.

The same eloquent precision is seen when the Quran addresses the muslims in the following terms:

> "Remember Me, then, and I will remember you."
> **The Cow,** 152

The Quran, however, speaks differently to the jews:

> "Children of Israel remember that I bestowed favours on you"
> **The Cow,** 40

The reason zehind this is the materialistic zent of the jews who remember God only in circumstances of benefit, interest, or favour. The muslims are spiritually more elevated and understand what it means to remember God for His own sake and not for an expected favour from Him.

In the same vein, God addresses the elite among the knowledgeable and wise:

> "So fear Me, you that are endowed with understanding."
>
> **The Cow,** 197

But when the Quran speaks to common men, it has this warning:

> "Guard yourselves against that fire whose fuel is men and stones, prepared for the unbelievers."
>
> **The Cow,** 24

Ordinary men can only be deterred zy the threat of Hell-fire but the elite know that God is infinitely more powerful than any fire and that, in fact, He can make such fire cool and harmless for whomever He pleases.

Accurate choice of words in the Quran is exemplified in Eblis's oath to tempt humanity:

> "I swear by Your Exaltedness that I will seduce all men,"
>
> **Sad,** 82

In swearing by God's Exaltedness in particular, and by no other divine attribute, Satan'proves his knowledge and cunning; for this particular attribute declares that God is absolutely in no need of His creatures: hence, those who believe or disbelieve are perfectly free to pursue the course they have chosen. Their actions would not affect God at all since He is the Trascendent Almighty who does not need His creatures or, for that matter, the entire universe.

in a Divine Utterance, God says:

"Those are in Hell and I care not and those in Paradise and I care not."

This follows from divine Exaltedness and it is the only loophole through which Satan can reach men. He can misguide and insinuate evil into them because God will not compel any one who preferred infidelity to become a believer. This is why the devil swore by God's Exaltedness when he declared his design to seduce men.

The devil also reveals his intelligence when he says:

> "I will waylay your servants as they walk on Your straight path, and spring upon them from the front and from the rear, from their right and from their left,"
>
> **The Heights,** 16

He mentions four directions of attack on men but neglects two: from above and from below. This is significant; above men there is divine Lordship and below them there is creaturely humility. Anyone who is devoted in humility to worship and serve the Exalted God will be immune against the insinuations of the devil.

Eblis specifies that his chosen seat of seduction will be on the straight path, on the road to the good, on the prayer mat. That person who neglects prayers, gets drunk, or is addicted to lechery has no need of a devil to lead him astray; his own soul has already done the trick. He has become a ruined human being and Eblis is a sharp thief who does not relish wasting his time over ruined houses.

Instances of eloquent Quranic accuracy of expression are inexhaustible. We find yet another one in the way the mention of forgiveness and mercy precedes that of punishment and wrath. God is first spoken of in the Fatiha (Opening verse of the Quran) as the Compassionate and the Merciful and then as 'the King of the Day of Judgment'. He is invariably described as pardoning whomever He pleases and then punishing whomever He wills. Forgiveness, thus, always comes before punishment except in two verses. The first concerns the amputation of the thief's hand:

> "He punishes whom He wills and forgives whom He pleases."
> **The Table,** 40

This punishment takes place in worldly life but is followed by forgiveness in the hereafter.

The second verse narrates Jesus's address to God on Judgment Day about the polytheists who worshipped him rather than God. He says to his Lord:

> "They are your bondsmen: it is for you to punish or to forgive them. You are the Mighty, the Wise One."
> **The Table,** 118

Jesus does not address God as the Forgiver and the Merciful out of deference and he mentions punishment before forgiveness to indicate the gravity of the transgression committed.

Quranic precision reaches the summit in the treatment of time. The Creator speaks about future events in the past tense. All the happenings of Doomsday are described in the past tense:

> "The Trumpet was sounded"
> **The Cave,** 99

> "The sky was rent asunder on that day, frail,"
>
> **The Inevitable,** 16
>
> "Hell was revealed to the erring."
> **The Poets,** 91
>
> "They were ranged zefore thy Lord."
> **The Cave,** 48

The reason for this treatment is that all events past and present have already taken place in God's Prescience; God is not limited by time so that the future can ze veiled from Him. He, the Exalted, is transcendent to both space and time. That is why we find certain Quranic phrases speaking simultaneously in two tenses in what appears to be a contradiction:

> "The Judgment of God has come: do not seek to hurry it on."
>
> **The Bee,** 1

The Judgment, according to the tense of the first clause, has already occurred in the past; God, nevertheless, orders men not to hurry it on as if it were still an event expected in the future. The secret behind this, as I explained, is that the Juegment has, in fact, occurred and ended in God's Prescience but has not yet unfolded before men's knowledge. There is no contradiction here but accuracy, precision, resourcefulness, and truthfulness in the rendering of profound meanings. These are deep mysteries that need to be studied.

All the previous examples illustrate the precise structuring and extreme accuracy of Quranic expression. The words are meticulously chosen and even the letters are meaningfully used. No addition, elision, advancing, or retarding occurs but by careful design. This approach is unequalled in any human composition. It is only found in the Quran.

As for the scientific hints and allusions to the wonders of natural phenomena that we find in the Quran and that reveal secrets and mysteries discovered only in our own age but quite unknown to Muhammad, peace be upon him, we devote another discussion; for this is a lengthy matter, indeed.

XII

The Quran Did Not Come From A Human!

I resumed talking to my friend:

Our discussion today of the scientific hints in the Quran may be more stimulating to your 'scientific' mind than our previous exchange. Modern astronomy, biology, anatomy, and atomic researches were certainly non-existent when some Quranic verses were revealed more than one thousand four hundred years ago to touch upon natural phenomena (or signs – **Ayat** – as they are called in the Holy Book). These verses deal with the sky, the earth, the stars, the planets, the development of the embryo, and the creation of man in a manner that corresponds to the latest discoveries of the sciences of our time.

The Quran did not tackle these subjects in the detailed approach of a specialized scientific text. It was primarily revealed as a book of creed, way of life, and legislation. Had it dealt elaborately and expressly with such topics, it would have shocked the Arabs of its time with things they could not comprehend. It resorted, therefore, to suggestions, hints, and intimations leaving them to be explained hundreds of years later zy the sciences and discoveries of the future and to manifest their real nature one generation after the other as miracles and signs which prove that the Quran is indeed from the True God.

God says in His Book:

> "We will show them Our signs in all the regions of the earth and in their own selves, until they clearly see that this is the truth."
>
> **Fussilat, 53**

Since those addressed were not satisfied with God's own testimony to the truth of the Quran, it became necessary that He prove it to them with manifest signs. The Quran continues day after day to uncover more of these amazing signs before our astonished eyes.

It mentioned in unequivocal terms the roundness of the earth employing, in the following verse, the verb **Yokawwer** (to round) twice to describe how the night and day 'slide upon' each other as two halves of a ball:

> "He causes the night to succeed (**Yokawwer**) the day and the day to succeed (**Yokawwer**) the night."
>
> **The Troops, 5**

Consider also in the same connection the verse which speaks about the 'spreading' of the earth where the verb **dahaha** is used to express this fact: 'After that, He spread the earth (**dahaha**)' (The Soul-Snatchers, 20). **Daha** is the only word in Arabic that means to spread something and to make it oval at the same time. The earth, as is well-known, appears to those who live on it spread flat but it is, in reality, round or, to be exact, oval in shape.

We read, in the Quran, another clear hint to the effect that the mountains 'swim' in space which, consequently, implies that the earth moves in space since both it and the mountains are one mass:

> "You see the mountains deeming them firm while they pass away like clouds."
>
> **The Ant,** 88

This means that the mountains which appear solid and inert really 'float' in space. Likening mountains to clouds, moreover, contains another very important suggestion about the 'fragile' structure of matter which, as we know today, is really composed of atoms just as the clouds are composed of droplets.

One of the striking things in the Quran is the frequent mention of the 'simultaneity' of night and day which co-exist in time from the beginning of creation to its end without each of them preceding the other:

> "The sun is not allowed to overtake the moon, nor does the night outpace the day."
>
> **Ya Sin,** 40

This clearly hints to the roundess of the earth. Night and day started simultaneously together since the beginning of creation as 'hemispheres'; if the earth had been flat, day and night would have succeeded each other by necessity. This suggestion is emphasized by another verse which speaks of the occurrence of Doomsday while the earth is, as it ever has been since its creation, passing through night and day at the same time:

> "When the earth has taken on its ornaments and was embellished, and

> its people deem they are masters of it, Our commandment comes zy night or by day and We make it waste as if it had not flourished yesterday."
>
> **Jonah, 24**

The pharse 'by night or by day' brings out that simultaneity of the two which can only be explained by the fact that one half of the planet is hidden from the sun and is, therefore, dark while the other half faces the sun and is lighted by its rays. If the earth had been flat, it would have been in one condition only at a time and it would have been incorrect to say, in the words of the Quran, 'nor does the night outpace the day.'

Linked to this observation is the mention, in the Quran, of the multiplicity of 'rising' and 'setting' points. God is described as the 'Lord of the rising-places and the setting-places' (The Ascending-Stairways, 40) and the 'Lord of the two Easts and Lord of the two Wests' (The Merciful, 17). If the earth had been flat, there would have been only one rising-point or 'east' and one setting-point or 'west'. On the Judgment Day, man says to the devil who accompanied him throughout his life:

> "Would we were as far apart as the two horizons (literally, the two Easts)."
>
> **Ornament, 35**

The Arabic text can be interpreted to indicate that the sun's setting in one area or horizon (west) can be the point of its rising in another area (east). This is only possible if the earth is round.

We find in the Quran references to paths or ways in the heavens:

> "By the heaven full of paths."
> **The Winds,** 7

We also find significant allusions:

> "By the sky with its returning of (rain)."
> **The Morning Star,** 11

The sky, that is, returns all that rises to it from the surface of the earth back again to that surface: it sends back the water vapour in the shape of rain, it holds rising bodies back by the force of gravity, it bounces back radio signals by deflecting them in the ionosphere, and it similarly deflects infra-red rays back to the earth's surface warming it at night.

Just as the sky returns and deflects back all that rises to it from below, it also deflects, absorbs, or scatters away all that is directed to it from space thus protecting the earth's surface from bombardments of the deadly infra-red or 'cosmic' rays. It acts exactly as a 'roof':

> "We spread the sky like a canopy and provided it with strong support,"
> **The Prophets,** 32

> "We have built the heaven with Our might, and We expand its vastness".
> **The Winds,** 47

The last words describe what is now known as the theory of the progressive expansion of the universe.

When the Quran was revealed, the smallest known unit of matter was the atom described as an individual, indivisible entity. The Holy Book came to speak of even more minute units into which the atom can be divided. It was, indeed, the first book ever to mention something smaller than the atom:

> "Not an atom's weight in heaven or earth escapes Him; nor is there anything smaller or greater but recorded in a Book Glorious."
>
> **Sheba,** 3

All these Quranic hints and suggestions are clear-cut references to such facts as the roundness of the earth, the nature of the sky, and the atom – facts that could not have been thought of by a sane or even madman in that age in which the Quran descended to the earth.

Consider, for instance, the insight given by the Quran into the embryo's evolution and its indication that the male sperm alone is responsible for the determination of the baby's sex:

> "He created the sexes, the male and the female, from a drop of ejected semen,"
>
> **The Star,** 45

This is a biological fact that has become known only in our own time. We say nowadays that it is the upper tip or 'head' of the sperm that solely carries the sex determination factors.

One of the phenomena that God brings forward as a challenge to those who deny resurrection is the shaping of the human finger with the formation of the finger-prints:

> "Does man think We shall never put his bones together again? Indeed, We can remould his very finger-tips".
> **The Resurrection,** 3–4

God stresses that He will even re-constitute the human finger, as part of the resurrection, restoring its original shape. This is a reference to the miraculousness observed in the peculiar make-up of finger-prints so that no two of them are alike.

The Quran describes the spider's web or 'dwelling' as the frailest of 'houses'. It did not say the spider's filament but 'dwelling'. It is now known that the filaments of the spider's web are four times stronger than similar filaments of steel. The weakness, according to the Quran, is in the 'dwelling' not the material of which it is made. The spider's dwelling, in fact, is the worst possible place for anyone seeking residence or protection. It is a trap for all outsiders and it is a slaughter-house for its own inhabitants: the female spider swallows its mate after fertilization, it also gobbles up its offspring after they are hatched, and the young spiders themselves devour each other.

The spider's dwelling is certainly the most vivid and eloquent example that can be employed to illustrate the worst kind of shelter or fate. Those who resort for help or protection to others than God will be opting for a kind of succour identical to that one may receive in a spider's dwelling. Hence, the expressiveness of the verse:

> "Surely the spider's is the frailest of all dwellings, if they but know it."
> **The Spider,** 41

The last words – 'if they but know it' – are significant; for they indicate that such knowledge about the frailty of the spider's dwelling will come to light only ages later just as the other biological mysteries referred to by the Quran.

In the sura called 'The Cave', we read this verse:

> "They stayed in their cave three hundred years and nine more."
>
> **The Cave,** 25

We now know that three hundred years in the solar calendar exactly equal three hundred and nine in the lunar – to the day, minute, and second.

In the sura of 'Mary', God – Exalted He be – narrates how Mary, when in labour, took shelter beside the trunk of a palm-tree wishing that she were dead:

> "And when the throes of child-birth drove her to the trunk of the palm-tree, she said: 'Would that I had died ere this and become a thing of naught, forgotten!' Then a voice cried out to her from below her:
>
> 'Grieve not. Your Lord has placed a brook running at your feet. And shake the trunk of the palm-tree toward you. It will drop fresh ripe dates in your lap."
>
> **Mary,** 23–5

Why, one wonders, was she called upon to eat of the ripe dates of the palm-tree? The latest scientific study provides the answer: ripe dates contain a styptic substance, oxytocin, which facilitates delivery by astringing the uterus and which helps to prevent hemorrhage after it. Ripe dates contain a laxative material and it is well-known that asperients of plant origin are useful in easing childbirth and making it safe by cleansing the colon. The prescription of ripe dates and the timing of their consumption with the 'throes of childbirth' reveal a remarkable scientific accuracy which, in fact, is not strange to the Quran.

It was such scientific, figurative, and literal truth that God referred to when He thus described the Quran:

> "Falsehood cannot come at it from before or behind."
> **Fussilat,** 42

> "If it had not come from God, they could have surely found in it many contradictions."
> **Women,** 82

The contradictions meant here are both among the verses themselves and between them and the established scientific truths discovered by the sciences. Both kinds of discrepancy invariably plague works of human origin. More often than not we find the writer anxious to add, omit or emend every time he produces a new edition of a book of his. We observe, in science, how theories succeed each other with the latter one exploding the former. However careful the writer may be, he is bound to fall into contradictions. This is a defect from which the Quran is free.

Moreover, the Quran is a miracle on another level: it tells of a past that has not been recorded in history and about a future which, at the time of Revelation, has not yet materialized. Its various prophecies have come true. About the victory of the Eastern Roman Empire after its defeat at the hands of the Persians, the Quran has the following to say:

> "The Romans have been defeated in a neighbouring land. But in a few years they shall gain victory."
> **The Romans,** 2–4

'Few' in Arabic indicates a number between three and nine; the Roman victory came seven years after their defeat. The Quran similarly predicted the muslim victory at Badr:

> "Their (the infidel's) army shall be routed and put to flight."
> **The Moon,** 45

It also prophesized their victorious entry into Mecca:

> "God has fulfilled the vision He showed to His messenger in very truth. You shall indeed enter the Sacred Mosque, by God's will, secure, (having your hair) shaven and cut, not fearing,"
> **Victory,** 27

Both events actually took place.

The Quran contains prophecies which we still see being realized in our own day; Ibrahim prayed to his God:

> "Lord, I have settled some of my offspring in a barren valley near your Sacred House, so that they may observe true worship. Put in the hearts of men kindness towards them, and

> provide them with the earth's fruits so that they may be thankful."
>
> **Abraham,** 37

He was calling for sustenance to be provided for that infertile, dry valley. Later on, God promised prosperity and wealth for the inhabitants of Mecca when they expressed fears that His injunction to prohibit the idolators from visiting the Ka'ba would result in losses and economic stagnation (the Mecca 'boom' depended on pilgrims). God answered the Meccans thus:

> "If you fear poverty, God, should He please, will enrich you through His bounty."
>
> **Repentance,** 28

This promise is being fulfilled nowadays before our own eyes in the form of oil that flows almost without end from the depth of the deserts with its prices shooting up madly sky-high one day after the other. It is equally fulfilled in the treasures of uranium deposits hidden in those deserts and ensuring the prosperity of the Arab countries to the end of time.

The Quran also talks about the mysteriously hidden world of the Unseen, of the secrets of the jinn and the angels which were only imparted to a few chosen souls among the sufis. If those blessed spirits see anything, they see only what accords with the words of the Quran. They only read what corresponds to its secrets.

The Quran delivers to us the final word in politics, ethics, systems of government, war and peace, the economy, society, marriage, and human relationships. It laid down perfect laws that anticipated and excelled, in the relevant areas, those included in the Universal Declaration of Human Rights, for instance. All this is presented in a unique style, a sublime phrasing, and a stylistic and aesthetic structure that stands apart in the history of the Arabic language.

When the mystic Ibn 'Arabi was asked about the secret of the miracle of the Quran, he replied in one phrase: 'Absolute truthfulness'. The words of the Quran are absolutely true whereas the utmost that any writer can achieve is to attain 'relative truth'; the most he can aspire to is to reach truth according to his own vision. The extent of an individual's vision, however, is always limited and it changes form one time to another. Everyone of us comprehends only one side of truth and misses many: we look at an angle and neglect others. The truth we reach is always relative. Only God possesses omniscience and comprehensive insight. He alone is capable of knowing the absolute, unchanging Truth. For this reason we say that the Quran is from God because it hit on the abolute truth with regard to everything.

Muhammad, peace be upon him, was asked to describe the Quran. He said: 'In it there is the history of what came before you, the judgment concerning your own affairs, and mention of what will come after you. It is the perfect Book and God's strong rope. It is the Straight Path. Any tyrant who deserts it will be broken down by God. Anyone who seeks guidance elsewhere will be led astray by God. It is never indistinct to the tongue nor are minds misled by it. Its freshness is not staled by repetition. Scholars never have their fill of it. Its wonders are never over."

This is our Book, my friend.

For all these characteristics, it could not have been composed by a human.

XIII

Doubts

My friend resumed his arguments:

You claim that the Quran never contradicts itself. Well, consider the follwing. The verse: 'Let him who will, believe in it, him who will, deny it' (The Cave, 29) is contradicted by another: 'Yet you cannot will except by the Will of God' (Man, 30). The Quran says that guilty men will be questioned on the Judgment Day:

> "That which they assert will be taken down. They shall be questioned."
> **Ornament,** 19

> "It is an admonition to you and to your people. You shall be questioned all."
> **Ornament,** 44

Yet, elsewhere it has this to say:

> "The wrong-doers shall not be questioned about their sins."
> **The Story,** 78

The wrong-doers, according to the Quran, will be known by their looks and 'they shall be seized by their forelocks and their feet'.**The Merciful,** 41

At one place the Quran makes it known that on the Day of Judgment no one will bind the guilty for punishment:

> "No one will be bound as he will bind."
>
> **The Dawn, 25**

According to my understanding, this means that every evil-doer will undertake his own punishment. The Quran says: 'Your own soul shall on this Day call you to account.' (The Night Journey, 14). In another place, however, we find this verse:

> "then fasten him with a chain seventy cubits long."
>
> **The Inevitable, 32**

– I began to counter his doubts:

What you have pointed out are not contradictions. Let us examine them together. 'Let him who will, believe in it, and who will, deny it' is an unambiguous verse indicating man's freedom of choice. This freedom, however, was not forcibly won form God. He gave it to us out of His own Will. This fact is pointed out in the second verse you quoted: 'Yet, you cannot will, except by the Will of God.'

Man's freedom falls within and not against God's Will. It can be exercised in a manner that contradicts what pleases God – as when we choose to disbelieve – but it cannot go against His Will. It is always exercised within that Will even if it contravened divine pleasure. This is a very fine point which we tackled in our discussion of free will and predestination. We said there that predestination by God is the same as the freedom of the human will; for God destines man to that which exactly corresponds to the content of his intention and heart. This means that He wants for man what man intentionally and freely wants for himself. Man, in fact, is predestined to what he has freely chosen. There is no compulsion, duality, or contradiction in this. Predestination **is** free will. This is indeed, one of the most difficult points in any attempt to solve the riddle of predestination and freedom of the will. What you describe as a contradiction is, ironically, the unravelling of this mystery.

As for the verses about the judgment of evil-doers, each one of them concerns a different group of persons. Some will be questioned and their testimony heard, others, whose myriad sins show on their faces, will be known by their looks and will be 'seized by their forelocks and their feet'. There will also be the hardened disbelievers against whom their own hands and feet will testify:

> "On that Day we shall seal their mouths. Their hands will speak, and their very feet will testify to their misdeeds."
>
> **Ya Sin,** 65

Certain wrong-doers will call their own souls to account tormenting them with sorrowful regrets and chastening them with grief. Those will be the ones whom no one binds but themselves. There will be, finally, those master criminals and tyrants who will even go to the extent of lying to God as they are brought before him and swear falsely in that dire situation:

> "On the Day when God restores them all to life, they will swear to Him as they now swear to you, and they will

fancy that they have some standing. Surely they are the liars."

She That Disputeth, 18

It is this group that will be put in long chains and dragged to Hell with the faces of its members looking shamefully down. It may be added here that Abu Hamed el-Ghazali interprets the chains spoken of in the Quran as the 'chains of causes' on which the criminals relied instead of God.

– My friend proceeded to ask me again: I would like to know your view on that 'Divine Knowledge' mentioned in such verses as the following:

"God alone has knowledge of the Hour of Doom. He sends down the rain and knows what every womb conceals. No mortal knows what he will earn tomorrow, no mortal knows where he will die."

Loqman, 34

The Quran affirms that such knowledge is God's alone and is not given to anyone else: 'He has the keys of all that is hidden. None knows them but He.' (Cattle, 59). Yet, any physician nowadays **can** know not only what is hidden in every womb but also whether that embryo is male or female. Scientists, moreover, are able to send down 'artificial rain' by certain chemical processes.

– The Quran, I replied, did not mention 'rain' – as you allude in your last remark – but **'gaith'** or a heavy, intense flood of rain that is sufficient to change the condition of an entire nation and save it by transforming its barrenness to fertility and prosperity (hence the Arabic **'gaith'** which literally means 'that which rescues'). Rain in such profusion cannot be brought down by any scientific process.

God's knowledge of what is concealed in wombs, on the other hand, is a total, comprehensive prescience and is not merely limited to the future baby's sex. It is a knowledge that concerns the destiny of that new creature, what he or she will be, what he or she will do in the world, and what his or her history from birth to death will be like. This, certainly, is a knowledge beyond the scope of any physician.

– My friend resumed his questioning: What about that 'Chair of God' which, you say, is vast enough to contain or comprehend the heavens and the earth? And what about 'God's Throne' which, according to your description, is 'carried by eight'?

– Your own mind, my friend, an insignificant human as you are in comparison to the universe, can comprehend the heavens and the earth. How can you, then, imagine that God's Chair will be incapable of containing them? The earth, the sun, the planets, the stars, and the galaxies are 'carried' in space by God's Power; how can you find it strange, therefore, that the Throne is described as being 'carried'.

– What is, then, the Chair and the Throne?

– Tell me what the electron is and then I shall tell you what the Chair is. Tell me what is electricity, what is gravity, what is time? In fact, you are not entitled to ask me about the nature of God's Chair or Throne because you do not know the essence of any single thing. The world is full of mysteries and those two belong to them.

– Very well, I wish you can so skilfully argue for the Quran's story about the ant that talked to warn off the rest of her race from the coming of Solomon's army:

> "an ant said to her sisters: 'Go into your dwellings, ants, lest Solomon and his warriors should crush you without knowing it."
>
> **The Ant,** 18

– If you had read even a little in entymology, you would not have asked about this phenomenon. Entymology literally teems with elaborate studies of ant and bee 'languages'. That the ants have a language is now a certain fact. It would have been impossible to distribute functions in a cell comprising hundreds of thousands of ants, to organize them, and to propagate orders and instructions among that huge mass without a means of communication or a language. There is nothing contradictory in that an ant recognized Solomon. Didn't man know the existence of God?

– Let me further enquire how is it possible that God wipes out what is written in His Tablet of Fate? It is said in the Quran: 'God confirms or abrogates what He pleases. His is the Eternal Book'. (Thunder, 39) Can your God make mistakes just as we do in our arithmetic calculations and go about blotting out and confirming? Or is it that He corrects himself as we, poor humans, do?

– God abrogates misdeeds by inspiring man with good actions. He says in His Book: 'Good deeds make amends for sins.' (Houd, 114). This is why he describes His good servants thus:

> "and We enjoined on them charity, prayer, and alms giving."
>
> **The Prophets,** 73

In this way we can understand how God abrogates without really blotting out in the bungling sense you implied.

– What do you say about this verse: 'I created mankind and the Jinn in order that they might worship me.' (The Winds, 56)? Is the Almighty in such dire need of our worship?

– On the contrary, **we** are the ones who desperately need to worship him. I ask you, do you adore beautiful women under orders? Don't you find a certain pleasure in such love? Aren't you transported into ecstasies when you taste your beloved's beauty? It is thus with God who is more Beautiful than any beautiful being we know or can imagine. If you knew **His Majesty, Beauty, and Exaltedness,** you would worship him finding in such reverence the zenith of elation and ecstacy.

Worship, as we see it, can only be based on knowledge. God can only be worshipped by being known. Knowledge of God is the end of all kinds of knowledge and the crowning of a long line of 'knowing' that starts from birth. The first thing a baby knows after he is born is his mother's breast; it is his first pleasure. The child, then, gets acquainted with his parents, his family, his community, and his environment. He starts to exploit that environment for his own use, turning it into another, new 'breast' supplying him with wealth, riches, and pleasures. He extracts gold and diamonds from the earth, pearls from the sea, fruits from nature. Such is his second source of pleasure in life after his mother's breast.

He then moves from knowing his earthly enviroment to exploring the heavens. He sets foot on the moon and launches his probes to Mars in a journey to the unknown thus enjoying an even more intense pleasure: that of discovering the universe itself.

That 'navigator' into space turns, however, to ask himself, "Who am I that I have come to know all this?" He thus starts a new journey of knowledge with his own self as target this time. He sets out to know himself, to control its capacities, and exercise them for his own good and for the benefit of others. This is a third kind of pleasure.

Following that, the summit of knowledge after acquaintance with the self is knowledge of God who created that self. With this final sort of knowledge man reaches the culmination of happiness for he comes to meet the Perfect, the Transcendent, the truly Beautiful above any beauty.

This is the pilgrimage of the worshippers to the worshipped on the road of reverence. It is all happiness. If there are hardships in life, it is because pricks must bleed the fingers of the rose pluckers. He who aspires to the summits of the infinite must toil to attain them. More marvellous and wonderful is the attainment by the worshipper to the knowledge of his God and the falling of the veils from his eyes. The mystic, clothed in rags, says, 'we live in such bliss that kings would fight us with swords for it, if they but know how it is.'

This is the sweetness of sincere worship; it is the worshippers' share. But God is in no need of such worship or of the entire creation. We do not adore him beacuse we are enjoined to do so but because we know His Beauty and

Grandeur. We do not find humiliation or subjection in worshipping Him but liberation and honour. We are liberated from all the enslavements of the world, from desires, appetites, ambitions, and money. As we come to fear God, we are no longer frightened by anyone else and we cower before no creature. Fear of God is courage, worshipping Him is freedom, humility before Him is dignity, and knowing Him is certainty.

Such is the nature of worship. We harvest its profits and pleasures. God is in no need of anything. He created us so that He may give and not take from us. He created us to invest us with some of his perfections. He is the All-Hearing and the All-Seeing and He gave us hearing and sight. He is the All-Knowing and the All-Cognizant and He gave us mind to take from His Knowledge and the senses to take from His Cognizance.

In a Divine Utterance, God says to His favoured servant:

> "My creature, obey me and I shall make you divinely-aided saying to a thing 'Be' and it becomes."

Wasn't that, in fact, what occurred to Jesus, peace be upon him? He resurrected the dead, created clay birds that came to life, and healed the blind and the leper – all by God's permission and aid.

Slavery to God, then, is the exact opposite of enslavement in the human sense. In the latter it means that the master exploits the slave's powers. In the former, however, it is quite the contrary: it is the Master who bestows endless gifts on His slave and invests him with infinite perfections.

When God says, 'I created mankind and the Jinn in order that they might worship me', this means in reality that He created men and Jinn only to grant and bestow on them love, goodness, dignity, and honour and to invest them with glory and vicegerecny on earth.

The Lord God, the Absolute, has no need whatsoever of our worship. We need such worship and all the boundless honour, goodness, and gifts it confers. He, of His Grace, permitted us to stand before His Presence at any time we wish without any previous appointment. He allowed us to stay in His presence as long as we desire and to call on Him as much as we can. This is realized as soon as we spread the prayer mat and open our prayers with **Allahu Akbar** (God is Greater). We are, then, in His presence and can ask of Him what we like.

Show me any king into whose chamber we can enter without previous notice and stay in his audience as long as we wish.

Maulana Sheikh Muhammad Metwaly el-Sha'rawy, a good man of God, has two beautiful lines of poetry on that divine gift:

> It is honour sufficient for me that I am a creature
> Welcomed without dates by my Master.
> Exlated He is in His Glorious Holiness,
> But I meet Him whenever I like.

Maulana el-Sha'rawy says also in this regard: 'Do you think that an artefact which is presented to its maker five times a day for inspection can malfunction?' He is referring, of course, to the five daily prayers.

These are but few, deep meanings of that verse which aroused your doubts:

> "I created mankind and the Jinn in order that they might worship me."

If you contemplated it carefully, it would have only aroused amazement and wonder in you.

XIV

Religion and Evolution

My friend said:

You are in a tight corner today; for you have to prove that the creation of man really occurred in the magical manner pictured by religion: the Creator moulding a piece of clay in His hand and breathing into it and, abracadabra, there is Adam! If you insist on adopting this view you will be sternly contradicted by the science of evolution which says your Adam came into being by a series of evolutions occurring to some animal forms. He is not, in fact, completely separated from his animal ancestry. He is, to be exact, a cousin of the apes sharing with them his seventh 'grandfather'. The unmistakeable similarity in the details of the anatomical structure of all these life-forms is evidence that they are all members of one family.

– I started to argue with him warming up for a heated scientific controversy:

Let me first of all correct your knowledge of the religious (Islamic) view of creation. God, according to that view, did not create Adam in a 'hocus-pocus' manner: here is a lump of clay, breathe in it and, voilà, there is the first man. The Quran presents a radically different account of Adam's creation. In that account, creation occurs in stages, phases, and over an extended time span measured in God's own scales. The

Quran did not say that man came directly out of clay but that he emerged from a 'race' or 'breed' (**solala**) that came from clay:

> "We created man from a breed (solala) of clay:"
> **The Believers,** 12

At the beginning man was nothing worthy of mention:

> "Didn't there pass on man a space of time when his life was a blank (insignificant thing)?"
> **Man,** 1

Man's creation, then, came in stages:

> "Why do you deny the dignity of God who has created you in gradual stages?"
> **Noah,** 13-4

> "We created you and gave you form. Then We said to the angels: 'Fall prostrate before Adam.' They all fell prostrate except Eblis who was not among the prostrate."
> **The Heights,** 11

> "Your Lord said to the angels: 'I am creating man from clay. When I have fashioned him and breathed of my Spirit into him, kneel down and prostrate yourselves before him."
> **Sad,** 71-2

These verses indicate that there were stages starting with the creation out of clay which was followed by formation, then fashioning, and, finally, breathing of God's Spirit into the creature: man. The word 'then' us'ed in this context, or the temporal dimension of the entire process, should be understood in relation to 'divine time'; it could mean millions of years:

> "Each day of His is like a thousand years of your reckoning."
> **Pilgrimage, 47**

God, exalted He be, defines the temporal phases of man's creation in the 'Prostration' sura:

> "He first created man from clay, then bred his offspring from a drop of despised fluid. He fashioned him and breathed into him of His Spirit. He gave you eyes and ears and hearts;"
> **The Prostration, 7–9**

At the beginning, it is clear, there was clay. Then came a race (**solala**) bred from semen or 'the despised fluid'. These were the early, humble origins of man or the 'blank' insignificant thing spoken of by the Quran. Man was then moulded and fashioned. After that the 'spirit' was breathed into him and he was, thus, endowed with hearing, sight, and 'heart' becoming Adam. The first man, therefore, emerged at the end of a series of evolutions and was not made instantaneously in the hocus-pocus style you imagine.

We read in the Quran: 'God brought you from the earth like a plant' (Noah, 17). This is a clear indication that creation was like the growing of a plant with all the evolutionary phases, time, and gradation that this process passes through. The real puzzle, however, concerns the exact nature of such phases or stages. Did the tree of life originate in its entirety from one source or 'parent'? This tree is basically of clay by virtue of chemical structure, and it is a fact that all its forms revert after death to their clayey origin. But by 'parent' we mean something more than the clayey origin. The question we want to pose is whether a primeval cell emanated from that primitive clay and multiplied to yield all those genuses and species of plants and animals including man; or whether there were various beginnings: one origin evolving into plants, another developing into such animal branch as the sponge for instance, a third from which fishes evolved, a fourth whose development yielded reptiles, a fifth from which birds emerged, a sixth forming the matrix for the evolution of mammals, and a separate beginning from which man evolved thus having an ancestor of his own like the other genuses?

The anatomic similarity among the branches, genuses, and species of the tree of life does not exclude the evolution of each genus from a distinct origin. Such anatomical similarity in all life forms, however, is evidence to the unity of their Maker because they are all fashioned out of one material, in one method, and according to one plan. This is the only necessary consequence of the similarity. But it does not inevitably follow from this fact that all life forms evolved from one origin.

Consider, in this regard, the similarity we observe in the means of transportation. The car, the train, the tram, and the diesel locomotive are all built round similar mechanical and structural principles indicating thereby that they are all inventions of the human mind. This, nevertheless, does not exclude the possibility that each one of them derived from an independent origin or from a separate engineering concept.

Moroever, it would be erroneous to say, for example, that the hand-cart spontaneously evolved by dint of laws inherent in it to become a horse-drawn carriage, an automobile, a steam locomotive, and a diesel locomotive in succession. The truth is that each of these inventions was realized as a result of a mental mutation in the inventor's mind and a creative leap in the engineer's. No one invention emerged from another though the temporal succession in which they appeared may lend credence to such view. What really happened was something else: every invention of the above started independently as a creative mutation in the inventor's mind.

This illustration throws light on Darwin's errors and the pitfalls and lacunae he fell victim to when formulating his theory.

Let us review what Darwin wrote in his **Origin of Species**. The first thing he discovered during his voyage on **The Beagle** was the identical anatomical plan on which all animal species were moulded. The skeleton, for example, is the same in most vertebrates. The arm in the ape corresponds to the bird's wing and that of the bat. Every piece of bone in it is matched by another in those wings with slight modifications to suit the function of the member. The bones in birds are thin, tender, light, hollow, and covered with feathers.

The long neck of the giraffe contains seven vertebrae: the same as in man's and as in the hedgehog's which is too short to be called a neck. Man's hand has five fingers and we find the same quinary formation in apes, rabbits, frogs, and lizards. Pregnancy lasts nine months in whales, apes, and human females, while sucking takes two years in the three species. The tail vertebrae in apes are found merged and telescoped in man's caudal bone or the coccyx. The tail muscles have changed in man into a solid bottom for the pelvis. The heart with its four chambers and the layout of the body's arteries and veins are identical in horses, donkeys, rabbits, pigeons, and men. The same similarity of structure is observed with regard to the digestive apparatus: the pharynx, the stomach, the duodenum, the small and the large intestines, and the anus, in that order. The genital apparatus is similar in all: the testicles, the ovary, and their ducts. The urinary apparatus is also common to all: the kidney, the uriter, and the bladder. The breathing system consists of the same components: the trachea or windpipe, and the two lungs. The lung in amphibians is the floating bag in fish.

In the light of all such correspondences it was natural for Darwin to conclude that all animals are members of one family scattered in and differentiated by various environments. Each species, according to his conception, adapted to its own environment. The whale in arctic zones developed a coat of fat while the bear put on one of fur. The skin of jungle man living under equatorial sun became black like a protective umbrella against the scorching rays. The eyes of cave lizards atrophied because useless in the dark and they became blind, while their prairie brethren still retain their sight. Those animals that took to the water developed their limbs into fins and those that took to the air evolved theirs into wings. Those destined to walk the earth transformed their limbs into legs.

Doesn't the embryo in fact, give the process away? At a certain stage of its development we find it breathing through gills. These, then, wither away and the lungs appear. At another stage it develops a tail which, in turn, disappears. At one time it is covered with hair which later on recedes.

Rock layers tell us, through the fossils they preserve, a concatenated story about the emergence and disappearance of one genus after the other: from simple mono-cell animals, to myriad-celled ones, to molluscae, to crustaceans, to fishes, to amphibians, to reptiles, to birds, to mammals, to man.

Darwin was right, in fact he was a genius, when he laid down that invaluable premise of anatomical similarity among animals. He was equally on the right track when he posited the hypothesis of evolution.

He fell into error, however, when he hazarded an explanation of the process of evolution and his conception of the phases and details of such process was mistaken.

For Darwin believed that evolution is solely motivated by latent materialistic factors. Animals fight with tooth and claw in a bloody and terrible struggle for survival. The weak are eliminated and survival is always for the fittest. Such war raging in nature is the power that picks out the strong and well-adapted creatures fostering them, preserving their offspring, and opening up before them the vistas of life.

This theory may explain the survival of the stronger but it does not account for that of the beautiful. A pied wing has no more physical advantages or survival value than a plain, white one. It is certainly no more efficient in flight. If we grant that a male seeking for mate prefers one with a pied wing, a question will immediately arise as to the reason for this since the variegated colours do not represent any increment in efficiency. If we include preference for the more beautiful in our estimation, as we are bound to do in the light of the previous question, the materialistic interpretation collapses completely.

In the latter case the theory remains incapable of explaining why something like the horse should branch out of the donkey family, or why a beautiful, delicate and sensitive animal like the gazelle should evolve out of the ibex, although it is less strong and tough than members of that species. One wonders about the way in which that theory can account for the hoopou's wing, the peacock's feathers, and the amazingly spotted and wonderfully coloured types of butterflies. In such phenomena we discern the hand of a master artist inventing and creating. We are no longer in the realm of a crude and rough business like the war of survival and the struggle of tooth and claw.

The second error in the theory of evolution came at the hands of the advocates of 'mutation'. Mutations are new characteristics that unexpectedly appear in the offspring on account of incalculable changes occurring when the male and female cells join in mating and the chromosomes responsible for determining hereditary characteristics cross with each other.

Sometimes the new characteristics may be detrimental in the case of deformities and disfigurements. At other times, however, the mutations may be useful and appropriate for the animal's new environment. An animal that takes to the water, for example, may develop flat feet. This new characteristic is certainly beneficial; for such type of feet is more suitable for swimming. Nature, then, fosters this characteristic. It transmits it to the new generations and, at the same time, weeds out the older feature because of its inappropriateness. In this way, evolution from ordinary to membraneous legs takes place.

This thory erred when it established evolution on the basis of haphazard mutations and mistakes. It totally overlooked any element of planning or creativity. Chance mutations can never be valid bases for an explanation of the inventiveness, accuracy, and precision we observe in everything around us.

A mosquito, for instance, lays its eggs in a swamp. Miraculously, it seems, every egg comes into being equipped with two bags to help it to float. From what quarter, one wonders, did the mosquito learn Archimedes'laws so that it equipped its eggs with those floating bags? Consider also those desert trees that produce 'winged' seeds which fly for miles with the wind and are spread over vast areas. In what school did these trees know enough about aereal lift laws to enable them to make such winged seeds that fly hundreds of miles in search of suitable grounds for growth?

There are, again, those 'carnivorous' plants that equip themselves with snares and remarkable 'booby traps' to catch and swallow up insects. With what mind were they able to devise these tricks?

In such examples we are, in fact, before a Comprehensive Mind that thinks and invents for His creatures all sorts of ways and means. Evolution is unthinkable without that Creative Mind:

> "He that gave all creatures their distinctive form and then rightly guided them."
>
> **Ta Ha,** 50

The third difficulty facing Darwin's theory is the recently discovered chromosome or gene chart. It is now known that every animal species has a chromosome chart peculiar to it alone. It is impossible that any species did or could evolve from another because of the difference in chromosome charts.

We conclude from the previous review that Darwin's theory is shaken. Although anatomical similarity among animals and evolution itself are widely accepted facts, the stages and the nature of the latter process are still a mystery. Were there separate beginnings for the various genuses or do they all go back to identical origins?

Evolution is clearly mentioned in the Quran just as the stages of creation, formation, fashioning, and breathing of spirit are. Science, however, has not yet been able to formulate a valid theory that can explain these stages.

If we go back to the 'Prostration' sura, we will find the following account of creation:

> "He first created man from clay then bred his offspring from a drop of despised fluid. He fashioned him and breathed into him of His Spirit. He gave you eyes and ears and hearts;"
> **Prostration, 7–9**

The meaning is quite clear: those early origins of man from which Adam later evolved and which procreated by means of a 'despised fluid' had no hearing or sight or 'heart' (in the sense of mind or reason). These faculties evolved later on when the spirit was breathed into Adam in the last stage of his 'moulding'. Such origins, then, could have been some forms of undeveloped animal life. We remember again in this context the verse:

> "Didn't there pass on man a space of time when his life was a blank (insignificant thing)."
>
> **Man,** 1

The truth, in spite of all, still remains an unsolved riddle. No one can claim that he has attained it. What really occurred in creation may have been totally different from our own views and those of scientists. The entire subject continues to be open for investigation. All that science has ventured so far are guesses.

XV

'There Is No God But Allah'

My friend said:

Don't you agree with me that you over do the use of the phrase 'there is no god but Allah' as if it were a key that opens every door? You bury your dead and receive your new-born babies while repeating this phrase. You engrave it on seals, decorate necklaces with it, print it on coins, and hang it on walls. You say that whoever pronounces it from your number will have his body saved from Hell¿fire. If any one utters it a hundred thousand times, he will go the Paradise, as if it were a magic talisman, a charm to scare the jinn away, or fairy tale bottle for holding giants captive.

There is, moreover, those mysterious letters with which many Quranic suras open and which have no apparent meaning for you: A.L.M., K.H.Y., A.S., T.S.M., H.M., A.L.R., etc.

Will I escape torment if I uttered 'there is no god but Allah'? Well, if yes, then I hereby utter it in your presence as a witness along with those who are present with us today: 'There is no god but Allah'! Is it all over now?

– You have not said anything, my friend.

This phrase benefits those who act its meaning out, it is not for those who pronounce it with the tip of their tongue. It implies a method of action and a life plan; it is not just the aggregate of some letters. Let us study its meaning. When we say 'there is no god but Allah' we really mean that none is to be worshipped except God. Our entire creed can, in fact, be found in the negator **la** (no) and the exceptive **illa** (but), in the negation and affirmation that both words indicate. Between negation and affirmation lies our whole creed.

'La' denies divinity to anything. It denies it to all the worldly pleasures we worship: wealth, splendour, power, lusts, fine living, gorgeous women, luxurious affluence, pomp.. We refuse to be enslaved by these or worship them. We deny divinity to them. By 'la' we also restrain our own selves that desire them. For man is wont to worship his own self, his own opinion, prejudice, will and whim. He is naturally prone to adoring his intelligence, talents, and fame and imagining that with them he can control events and people and even the entire society around him. He, thus, deifies himself without knowing it. It is against such aggrandizement of self that we say 'no' or **la**; we refuse to worship or confer divinity on it.

We say 'no' to the director, to our superior, and to the ruler. We decline to accept them as gods, for 'god' here means an agent or doer and the true agent, in our belief, is God alone. All else are mere means or causes. We, therefore, say 'no' to the director, the minister, and the president; to wealth, splendour, power, and to the self with all its talents and intelligence. We refuse to confer divinity on them.

By '**illa**' (but), on the other hand, we except only One Being from the attitude outlined above, a Being with regard to whom we confirm such agency and potency: God.

Our entire creed falls between **la** and **illa**, between negation and affirmation, as I said. Anyone who is totally preoccupied with accumulating money, heaping wealth, flattering the rulers, ingratiating himself with superiors, seeking pleasures, following his prejudices and whims, narcissistically clinging to his opinions, and fanatically upholding his own viewpoint has not really said 'no' to all these objects of his worship. He is prostrating himself before their altar unknowingly. If he says 'there is no god but Allah', he is lying; he is merely uttering with his tongue that which he does not confirm by the actions of his limbs.

'There is no god but Allah' really means that there is no reckoner or observer except God. He alons is worthy of being feared and watched. Whoever fears sickness, the microbe, the policeman's baton, or the ruler's soldiers has not truly said 'no' to all such false gods. He remains in their service joining a host of fake gods with his Creator. He lies even if he utters 'there is no god but Allah'.

All this proves that 'there is no god but Allah' is a covenant, a constitution, and a way of life. It is intended to be enacted. To whomever acts according to its full implications, it really becomes a talisman opening all recalcitrant doors. It will save him in this and in the next world and will be his gateway to Paradise. A mere utterance of that phrase with the tongue without heart-felt belief or bodily actions confirming it is quite useless.

In addition, 'there is no god but Allah' expresses a philosophical attitude. Dr Zaki Naguib Mahmoud, the Egyptian writer on philosophy, says that this testimony implies the admission of three facts: that the utterer or witness exists, that the entity indicated by the witness exists, and that the persons before whom the testimony is delivered also exist. It is, to put it more simply, a clear admission that the self, God, and the others have a real existence.

Islam, thus, rejects both philosophical idealism and materialism. It repudiates both the right and the left choosing for itself a mediate position. It rejects philosophical idealism because it does not recognize the existence of others or that of the objective world as an external fact independent of mind. Everything, according to this philosophy, occurs in the mind just like dreams or thoughts. You, as a person, the radio set, the street, society, the newspaper in my hand, and all the wars around us are only events or visions that take place in mind. The external world does not really exist.

This extremist idealistic postion is rejected by Islam and denied by the testimony of 'there is no god but Allah'; for that testimony, as I said, is a frank admission that the witness, the entity attested for, and those present when it is delivered – the self, God, and others– are all accepted facts.

Islam similarly rejects philosophical materialism because that creed accepts only the objective world and denies anything beyond it; it denies the unseen and God.

In this attitude, Islam advances a realistic philosophy and manner of thinking. It recognizes the existence of the objective world and, then, adds to that world all the magnitude that the unseen existence of God confers. It presents, in fact, a synthetic structure combining the ideas of both left and right within a comprehensive philosophy that still challenges the efforts of thinkers by surpassing their probabilistic theories which are not established on any certainty.

The testimony of 'there is no god but Allah', then, implies a way of life and a philosophical stance. As a materialist, you my friend, lie twice when you utter that testimony. Firstly, you are admitting what your materialistic philosophy denies. Secondly, you do not act according to the implications of the testimony even for one second of your life.

As for the mysterious letters – A.L.M., K.H.Y. 'A.S., H.M., A.L.R., etc – let me ask you first about the y's and x's in algebra, the logarithms, and the energy equation: $E = mc^2$. All these are mystifying riddles for anyone who is ignorant of mathematics and algebra. For those, however, who are well¿versed in such studies, they carry very important meanings. In a similar manner, the Quranic letters will be found to have profound significance when their meanings are revealed to us.

– My friend interrupted sarcastically:

And have their meanings been divulged to **you?**

– I replied dropping a bombshell:

This is a very interesting subject. It needs a lengthy exposition which may amaze you.

XVI

K.H.Y.'A.S.

– I said to my atheist interlocutor:

You must have been startled the first time you read those separate letters at the opening of some Quranic suras. I mean such clusters as: H.M., T.S.M., K.H.Y. 'A.S., K., S., and so on. I wonder what did you say to yourself then.

He just pouted his lips indifferently muttering indistinctly:

3 Well!

– Well. what?

– Well, I thought that your prophet was merely impressing you with such trick.

– Very well, let us examine that 'nonsensical talk' with which you think our prophet tricked us.

Take, for example, a rather short sura like 'Qaf'. If we count the occurrences of the letter K (**Qaf**) in it, we will find that they are fifty seven. Consider the sura which follows it, **Counsel**, which is twice its length and opens also with the letter K. You will find that this letter occurs fifty seven times also. Is this a mere coincidence?

If we add up those occurrences of the letter K, we will have a hundred and fourteen: the number of the suras which the Quran contains. Do you remember how the sura of Qaf opens and how it ends? It begins: 'K. By the glorious Quran' and ends with the verse: 'Admonish with this Quran whoever fears My warning'. These are more like hints indicating that K (Qaf) symbolizes the Quran. Remember that the letter K occurs a hundred and fourteen times in both suras which, as I said, is the number of the Quran's suras:

– My friend said nonchalantly:

These are just coincidences.

– I continued calmly:

Let us continue our probing. Feed all the Quran's suras into a computer and instruct it to give us some statistics on the average occurrence of the K letter in them.

– He became totally alert and tensely attentive saying:

Has this been already done?

– I replied quietly: Yes, it has.

3 What was the result?

– The computer informed us that the highest averages and rates occur in the Qaf sura. This sura is mathematically "superior" to all others in the Quran with regard to this particular letter. Is this another coincidence?

– How strange!

– The 'Thunder' sura opens with the letters A.L.M.R.; we fed this into the computer and it gave us an account of the occurrence frequency of these letters in the sura:

A.	occurs	625 times.
L.	occurs	476 times.
M.	occurs	260 times.
R.	occurs	127 times.

Thus the letters' frequency of occurrence is in the same descending order in which they are ranged at the sura's beginning: A.L.M.R.

The computer, then, worked on the averages of these letters' occurrences in the Quran as a whole. It fed back to us the following bombshell: the highest rates or averages for these letters are in the Thunder sura which, with regard to them, is mathematically superior or preponderant to any other sura of the Quran.

The same thing happened in the statistics concerning the opening A.L. M. of the Cow sura:

A.	occurs	4592 times.
L.	occurs	3204 times.
M.	occurs	2195 times.

The frequency of occurrence is in the same descending order found at the opening of the sura: A.L.M. The computer further revealed that these letters have mathematical preponderance over others within the Cow sura. A similar ratio is found in 'The Imrans' which also opens with A.L.M.:

A.	occurs	2578 times.
L.	occurs	1885 times.
M.	occurs	1251 times

The same correspondence is observed between the descending order of frequency and that of occurrence at the opening of the sura. Likewise, these letters are found in this sura in a higher rate than the other letters of the alphabet.

The Spider sura opens with A.L.M. These letters are distributed in it in the following manner:

A.	occurs	784 times.
L.	occurs	554 times.
M.	occurs	344 times.

This is the same descending order of their occurrence at the opening of the sura. They are also found in it in a higher ratio than the other letters of the alphabet. The 'Romans' begins also with A.L.M. and these occur in the following frequency ratios:

A.	is found	547 times.
L.	is found	196 times.
M.	is found	318 times.

Again, this is the same descending order of their occurrence at the start. These letters have, as in the previous cases, a higher ratio of occurrence than any others of the alphabet in the same sura.

Among all the suras opening with A.L.M., we find that those revealed in Mecca are mathematically preponderant, with regard to the average frequency of occurrence of these letters, over the other Meccan suras. We also find that those suras revealed in Medina and beginning with the letters A.L.M. are similarly mathematically preponderant, with regard to the average frequency of these letters, over the other Medina suras.

The same phenomenon is observed in connection with the cluster A.L.M.S. which opens the 'Heights'. The computer informs us that the average occurrence frequency of these letters is highest in that sura which is mathematically preponderant in this regard over other Meccan suras.

In 'Ta Ha' it is found that 't' and 'h' occur in frequencies higher than in all Meccan suras. The same happens with the opening K.H.Y.'A.S. of 'Mary' where their average occurrence frequency is higher than in all Meccan suras.

The same results hold in the case of all the suras opening with the letters H.M. If these suras are put together, the occurrence frequency of the H.M. letters is found to be higher in them than in all Meccan suras. This fact applies also to the two suras beginning with S: Sad and The Heights (the last actually opens with A.L.M.S.). These two suras were revealed successively in this order. If they are taken together, they will be found to preponderate mathematically over all other suras of the Quran with regard to the average occurrence frequency of these letters with which they open.

A similar phenomenon is noted in all suras starting with A.L.R.; namely, Abraham, Jonah, Houd, Joseph, and Al-Hijr. Four of these were revealed in succession and if taken as a unit, computer read-outs on them will show the highest average of occurrence frequency for the letters A.L.R. among all Meccan suras. In 'Ya Sin' the same thing obtains but in reverse, as it were, with regard to the letter sequence Y.S. because the Y., the last letter in the Arabic alphabet or 'ya', comes before the S (sin). That is why we note that the frequency of occurrence for these two letters in this sura is, in fact, lower than in all other suras of the Quran whether revealed in Mecca or Medina.

My friend fell silent and I went on to reassure him by saying that I was not making up all these figures. As a matter of fact, I was quoting from a study by an Egyptian scientist, Dr. Rashad Khalifa, who lives in America. His book, **Miracle of the Quran,** (published in English by Islamic Productions International, St. Louis, Missouri), contains the details of his research. I presented that book to my friend. He leafed through it in silence and I continued my talk to him:

You see, it is no longer a question of chance. We are before precise laws and carefully calculated placing of letters each of which is weighed as if with an exacting scale. I read to you the appropriate verse from the Quran.

> "It is God who has revealed the Book with truth and justice."
>
> **Counsel,** 17

And what a sort of justice have we here! We are before such a finely just scale that it can weigh a hair or a letter. With findings like these the idea that the Prophet was the author of the Quran is no longer tenable. It is inconceivable to imagine him saying to himself in advance of composing the Quran, "I will fashion the Thunder sura on the letters A.L.M.R. and put in it the highest average of occurrence frequency for these letters in the entire book."

It is to be asked where could he have found anyone to undertake providing him with these statistical averages. Such a task can only be accomplished by an electronic computer. If the Prophet had attempted it himself, he would have undoubtedly spent several years just to calculate the letter dispositions for only one sura – adding and subtracting at the level of knowledge available in his age. He was not even aquainted with the knowledge of his age. It is to be further enquired whether he occupied himself with composing or with the calculation of the letter placements. We confront here an impossibility.

Moreover, if we take into consideration that the Quran was revealed in small, separate parts along a time span of twenty three years, we will certainly conclude that formulating advance statistical averages for its letters is another impossibility. It is a task of which the All-Knowing alone is capable. It is He who knows everything before it occurs and calculates swifter and more accurately than all imaginable computers combined. God alone, whose Knowledge has comprehended everything, can do this. The individual letters with which the suras open are only symbols of His Knowledge imparted by Him in His Book and left for us to discover as time goes by:

> "We will show them Our signs in all the regions of the earth and in themselves, until they clearly see that it is the truth."
>
> **Fussilat, 53**

I am not saying that what has so far been uncovered contains all the secrets of these letters. It is just a beginning that has been made; no one yet knows to what horizon will it lead us.

With the new significance now seen in such letters, the idea that the Quran had been composed can be completely and finally refuted. This significance puts us before accurate calculations and profound meanings for every letter so that no one dare allege that this is just mere scribbling. Can't you see, my friend, that you face here a species of language that cannot be described as just a string of letters?

My friend did not answer, but kept browsing through that book I gave him without uttering a sound.

XVII

The Miracle

My friend said:

– I don't pretend to understand how it is possible for the Merciful God – whom you describe as the Ruthful, the Benevolent, the Bounteous, the Oft-Pardoning, and the Remitter to command His Prophet and 'close friend' (**khalil**), Abraham, to slaughter his son? Don't you concur with me that this is rather difficult to believe?

– It is obvious from the context and events of the story that God's wish was not for Abraham to slaughter his son. The proof is that no such thing happened. Divine wish was that Abraham should 'slaughter' his excessive fondness and love for his son and deep attachment to him. It is impermissible that there should be any clinging in the heart of a prophet for any thing other than God: neither world, nor son or splendour or person. A prophet's heart should not be attached to any of these things. As is known, Ismail was born to Abraham in his old age and senility. He was, therefore, excessively fond of and attached to him. Hence, God's trial of His prophet was necessary. What the story narrates supports this interpretation. For when Abraham succumbed to his God's command and drew his knife to slaughter his son, the commandment came from heaven with the sacrificial lamb.

– What do you think, then, of Abraham's wonderful miracles such as his entry into fire and exit without being burnt? What have you also to say about the miracles that occurred to Moses when he transformed his staff into a serpent, or when he used the same staff to part the sea, or when he drew out his hand from under his armpit white as lily? Don't all these 'miracles' appear to you as a juggler's show in a circus? How can God go about proving His Omnipotence and Greatness by such acrobatics which are, in essence, instances of the irrational and of the contravention of natural order? Don't you say, in effect, that the strongest proof of God's Greatness is the order, reason, control, and laws which govern throughout the universe without being violated?

– Your understanding and conception of miracles are erroneous. You see them as juggler's tricks and irrational violations of law. The truth about them, however, is something else.

Allow me to use an illustration to clarify the matter for you. If you were destined to travel three thousand years back in time and enter upon Pharaoh in that bygone age with a transistor radio the size of a matchbox in your hand which 'sings and talks' all on its own, wouldn't he and his entire retinue be stupefied and damn the thing as a miracle, a work of magic, an irrational absurdity, or violation of all laws. We know now, however, that there are no such things in the innocent radio set. What actually happens in the transistors is governed by and unfolds according to the laws of electronics. It is, in fact, quite reasonable. It would be more amazing if you were to enter upon the king of Babylon with a television set in your hand showing pictures from Rome; and the Assyrian king would certainly clap his hands in wonder if you turned a plastic disc before his eyes and it started to talk.

Indeed, history records that when some colonialists arrived in Africa in a plane landing in the jungle among a crowd of primitives, the naked negroes fell prostrate on their faces, beat their drums, and sacrificed offerings thinking that God has descended from his heavens and that what had happened is a violation of all laws. We, on the other hand, know that an aeroplane flies and lands according to certain laws and that it is designed in line with precise engineering laws. Its flight in the air is a perfectly reasonable matter; it does not contravene the law of gravity. It transcends that law by another; namely, that of action and reaction. We are, in fact, dealing with a case of hierarchy of laws, and not with one where laws are violated. To give an example, we know that water climbs up inside the trunk of the palm-tree in an apparent violation of the law of gravity. It does not, in truth, contravene that law but acts in accordance with a group of laws which overrule gravity in that particular instance. These are the laws of the integrity of the water column, of capillarity, and of osmotic pressure. All of them act to draw the water up the palm-tree trunk.

Thus, we are never outside the pale of reason or of the rational. What occurred in miracles was not an acrobatic show. The stupefaction of the primitive negroes was due to their ignorance of such laws as governed the flight of the plane. Your own wonder at Moses's parting of the sea or turning the staff into a serpent, or at Jesus's raising of the dead, or at Abraham's harmless stay in fire are all of the same order as the primitives' amazement. You imagined that such miracles were irrational juggler's tricks and violations of law, while, in fact, they all occurred in harmony with divine laws which overrule the laws we are familiar with. Hence, they represent species of order and of the rational, but ones which are above our understanding. By such miracles God is not demolishing order but giving us a glimpse of higher order and laws and of the workings of a Mind too vast for us to comprehend.

Followers of the Baha'i sect have fallen into the same error you committed when they rejected miracles thinking that their acceptance is a contempt and degradation of reason. They resorted, consequently, to re¿interpreting the Quran by inventing other meanings for its words than those apparent. Moses, according to this view, did not really part the sea with his staff but the staff mentioned is the Law which parted or distinguished the true from the false. Similarly, his 'spotlessly' white hand is the symbol of benevolence; Jesus resurrected spirits not bodies and he opened minds not sightless eyes. In this way, those people played the trick of veering off the literal meanings of the Quran to allegorical and figurative interpretations and explanations whenever they met with anything **they** found inconceivable.

They took that course of action because they misunderstood the nature of miracles believing them to be, as you also saw them, irrational violations of law and contraventions of order.

As a matter of fact, we live now in an age in which miracles, if they occurred, would no longer be found inconceivable. We have seen science leading us to the surface of the moon. If human science gave us all this power, surely divine knowledge can grant us infinitely more.

Listen to this really beautiful verse:

> "Mankind and jinn: if you have power
> to penetrate the confines of heaven

and earth, then penetrate them! But this you shall not do except by our own authority."

The Merciful, 33

Authority here or 'power' is divine knowledge which is infinitely greater than that of man.

XVIII

The Meaning of Religion

My friend said:

3 Look, if there is really a Paradise as you say, I'll be the first one to enter it. For I am, indeed, more religious than many of those sheikhs of yours with their beards and rosaries.

– What do you mean by 'more religious'?

3 I mean I do not hurt anybody. I do not steal, kill, accept bribes, envy others, have grudges, or intend evil for any creature. I have only benevolence in my mind and my sole aim is general good. I wake up and go to sleep with an easy conscience and my motto in life is to reform things as best I can. Isn't this religion? Don't you say that the essence of religion is conduct?

– Ah, what you practice is something else called good manners. It is, indeed, enjoined by religion but is not symonymous with it. You are confusing religion with its requirements. Religion has only one meaning; namely, the knowledge of God; to know your God truly and to cultivate a certain conduct and behaviour towards Him. It is to know your God as He is – Supreme, Majestical, Near, Responding, All-Hearing, and All-Seeing. It is to pray to Him kneeling and prostrate in the reverence of creature to Creator. This private dealing between you and God is religion. As for your good conduct towards your fellow men, it is necessitated by religion and is, in fact, a God-oriented behaviour also.

Our Prophet, peace be upon him, said: "Alms reach the hand of God before that of the beggar". Whoever loves God will equally love his creatures and be charitable to them. If, however, your correct conduct and dealings are confined to men only recognizing and seeing nothing else beside them and this earthly life, you are a complete disbeliever be you ever so well-mannered in your behaviour with them. Indeed, your good manners in this case only prove your sharpness, your sense of propriety, and your tactfulness. They do not prove your religiosity. You simply want to win people, to succeed in life. Your good behaviour is merely a means to worldly gains. This is the bent of most disbelievers.

– Believe me when I tell you that sometimes I feel the presence of a power.

3 A power?

– Yes, there is an unknown power behind the universe. I fully believe that there is.

– What, then, is your conception of this power? Do you see it as a Being that sees, hears, understands, tends His creatures with guidance and care, sends them scriptures and messengers, and answers their calls and supplications?

3 Well, frankly, I don't believe in that conception. I don't even find it imaginable. Moreover, it seems to me naive and unworthy of that great power.

– Then it is a blind, electromagnetic power that drives the universe in a meaningless, amoral push towards nothing. This is the only appropriate description of your great power.

– May be!

– What a miserable view you have of your God. He gave you mind and you imagine him as an irresponsible fool. By God, you are certainly an atheist even of you well¿behaved to the end of time. All your good deeds will be rejected and thrown to the wind on the Day of Judgment.

– Won't this be injustice?

– Quite the contrary, it is justice itself. You thought that such deeds come out of your own self and have not been inspired by the Guiding and the All-Sage who led and guided you. It is you who are unjust to your god denying his favours. This is the difference, in fact, between the good deeds of the believer and those of the atheist in case both are equal in their external good manners and behaviour. Both may build a hospital for the treatment of the sick. The atheist says. 'I build this grand hospital for the people.' The believer, however, says, 'My God guided my efforts to build this big hospital for the people. I was only a means to the realization of this good.'

It is really a great difference. The latter person attributes the good deed to its real author and source leaving to himself only the role of means; and he is thankful to God for even this limited function praising Him for making him into a mediate cause. There is certainly a vast difference between pride and modesty, arrogance and humility, tyranny and meekness. That is why you do not pray or prostrate yourselves in your pagan creed of the electromagnetic power.

– Why should we pray? And to whom? I don't see any point in your prayers. Why all the various movements of the body, wouldn't piety of the heart have been sufficient?

3 The point and wisdom of prayers is that the false pride you dwell in be shattered the moment your forehead touches

the dust and your heart and tongue join in saying 'Exalted be my All¿Sublime God'. At this moment you will have finally realized your true position: you are the lower and He is the Supreme. You are dust walking on dust and He is a Being exalted over the seven firmaments.

As for your question about the necessity of bodily movements and why wouldn't heart-felt reverence be enough, let me ask in my turn: why was your body created in the first place? You are not satisfied with oral expressions of love but you desire to kiss and hug. You would mock anyone who is content with heart-felt generosity without giving out aid and money. God created the body so that it may expose what is hidden in your heart. What really fills your heart will overflow to your body. If your piety is sincere, it will show on your body making you kneel and prostrate yourself. If false, it will not go beyond your tongue.

3 Do you think that **you** will go to Paradise?

– We will all pass across Hell and then God will save those who feared Him. I don't know whether I have been a pious, God-fearing person or not. This is only known to the the Knower of the Unseen. All my deeds, regrettably, are mere ink¿blots on paper. The deed may be pure but the design may not. Intentions may be sound but sincerity may not. One may think that he is making good deeds for God's sake while he is really expending his efforts for the sake of fame and worldly glory among men. We often delude ourselves. We let illusions, wishful thinking, and false security take over us unconsciouly. We ask God for safety.

– Can any mortal be pure of heart in his devotion to God?

3 He can't be sincere out of his own will but it is God who

purifies hearts. That is the reason why the Quran speaks in most of the verses dealing with this matter about the 'purified' and not the 'sincere'. God, however, promised to guide to His own path those who 'return'; that is those who repent and revert to Him. So you have to return to Him and He takes over from that point.

XIX

'We Won Worldly Happiness, And You Got Delusions'

– My friend said with a note of joyous truimph:

We may disagree widely and argue for a long time. It is certain, however, that we come off the better from our fight with you. We won the happiness of this world while you emerge only with a few delusions in your heads. What is the use of talking when we have won the lion's share of this world's pleasures. We have enjoyed parties to the small hours, drinking, beautiful women, luxurious living and all sorts of pleasures untarnished by the taboos of the forbidden or **haram**. You, for your part, have only got your fasting, prayers, remembranec of God, and the fear of Reckoning. Who do you think is the real winner?

3 I am ready to concede that victory to you, if you have really gained your happiness as you say. If, however, we patiently consider the truth of the matter together, we will find that the picture you draw of happiness – midnight parties, drinking, pleasures unmolested by fear of the prohibition taboo – is truly misery in essence.

3 How is that?

3 Such life is, in truth, slavery to insatiable appetites that are no sooner satisfied than hunger again for more, and if

they are sated they grow dull and weary and you fall into torpor and sluggishness.

Are the embraces of women the right place to find lasting happiness in? We know that affections fluctuate, that passion is volatile, and that beautiful women are seduced by mere words of praise. The stories of lovers tell only of unhappiness which is exacerbated and crowned with greater disappointments if the infatuation ends in marriage. For in that latter estate each party will miss in the other the desired perfections he imagined were there. After the lust is slaked and the desire abates each will come to see the other's defects blown large as if through a magnifying glass.

What about great wealth? It is merely another form of slavery. The wealthy, in fact, are put in the service of their riches; they are enslaved in the process of aggrandizing, collecting, and guarding them thus becoming their servants in a reversal of the normal, or at least expected, course of events.

What about power and glory? Aren't they, in essence, pitfalls leading to arrogance and tyranny. The person in power is like a rider on a lion: today he has the reins in his hand but tomorrow he is eaten by the beast that carries him.

And are wine, drugs, gambling, lechery, and secret sex umhampered by fear of the unlawful, aspects of happiness? They are, in truth, but forms of escape from mind, from conscience, from the spirit's yearning and human responsibility by drowning oneself in the fire of lust and the rabidness of appetites. Is this really a higher style of life or a deterioration back to the hording of apes and the copulation of animals? The Quran has hit on the perfect truth when it described the 'unbelievers'.

> "The unbelievers take their fill of pleasures and eat as the beasts eat; but Hell shall be their home".

Muhammad, 12

It is not denied that the unbelievers enjoy their life; but this joy is like that of animals. Is it really a form of happiness? This life of lust is only a series of stimulated desires, tensions, consuming hunger, and gorging surfeit. It has no relation whatsoever to true happiness which can only be attained in a state of psychic peace and relief and of spiritual liberation from all kinds of slavery. In its final definition true happiness is a state of peace between man and his soul, the others, and God. This reconciliation, peace, and sense of internal quietude can only be reached through a certian expenditure of effort when man devotes his strength, wealth, and health to the service of others, when he lives in intention and deed a life of goodness and charity, and when his relationship with God is deepened by prayer and reverence reciprocated from the Divine by Help, Light, and Tranquility.

Such happiness is the essence of religion. Didn't the mystic in his rags cry out, 'We live in such bliss that kings would fight us with swords for it, if they but know how it is'. Those who tasted that bliss, the bliss of contact with God and peace with the self, know that the mystic is quite right.

— But weren't you just a few years ago 'one of us' drinking and painting the town red as we used to do? Didn't you express atheistic ideas in your book **God and Man** which outreached even the most disbelieving in its audacity? What set you on the opposite course?

3 God, may He be exalted, changes but is Himself not changed.

3 I know that you attribute everything to God's grace. But what was your role or effort in that transformation?

3 I looked round me and found that death and dust are absurd and meaningless jests. I saw the universe in which I live precisely and accurately governed with no room for aberration or disorder. If my life was meaningless and destined for nothingness, as the 'absurdists' imagine, why is it, then, that I weep, repent, or feel a burning yearning for truth and justice willing to sacrific my life and blood for such values.

I saw the stars moving in their orbs by law; communities of insects talking; plants seeing, hearing, and feeling. I saw that animals have "ethics"; that the human brain, the wonder of wonders, contains more than ten thousand million nerve connections all working at the same time in a miraculous perfection. If just one fault occurred here or there, it would immediately result in paralysis, blindness, loss of speech, mental confusion, or hallucination. Such defects, however, are only exceptional. What power, then, maintains the safety of this enormous machine and who endowed it with all those perfections?

I saw beauty in the leaves of trees, in the feathers of peacocks, and in the wings of butterflies. I heard delightful music in the chanting of hoopous and the chattering of birds. Wherever I turn my face I see the brush strokes of a painter, the designs of intelligence, and the creations of an inventive hand.

I observed in nature an integrated, accurately wrought structure in which everything coincidental or haphazard is impossible. Every phenomenon cries out, 'I have been planned by a designer and created by a Puissant Creator'.

I read the Quran and found in my ears a resonance and rhythm unknown in familiar language. It staggered my mind. It delivers the conclusive word in everything that it touches upon: matters of state, morals, legislation, the universe, life, the self, and society; and that in spite of its being revealed more than one thousand four hundred years ago.

The Quran accords with all that science discovered or invented although it was brought to the world by an illiterate bedouin from a backward nation which did not know the light of civilization. I read the history of that man and of his deeds, and I concluded that he was a prophet. He could not have been but a prophet and this wonderful universe could not have been created but by the Puissant God whom the Quran mentioned and described His works.

Having listened attentively to all I said, my friend spoke trying desperately to feel his way to a last breach through which he can demolish my arguments:

– What would happen if all your expectations are erroneous and you end up, after a long life I hope, in dusty death that has nothing beyond it?

3 I would not have lost anything! I would certainly have enjoyed as full, happy, and eventful a life as can be. It is you, however, who will lose much if my beliefs are right and my

expectations come true. I assure you, my friend, that they are true and that you will have a tremendous surprise.

While I was addressing him, I looked intently at his eyes and saw for the the first time a flood of terror flowing from them. His lids were twitching and convulsing.

It was, however, a transient moment of fear. He soon regained his composure. But this was enough for me to realize that for all his arrogance, obstinacy, and obduracy he was standing precariously on the edge of a precipice of doubts, emptiness, and nihilism clutching at nothing.

3 He resumed talking in a voice that he endeavoured to charge with certainty:

You shall see that dust is all that awaits us or you.

– Are you sure of that?

And for the second time terror flooded his eyes.

– Yes.

He replied stressing every sound of the word as if in fear that his accent may give him away.

3 You are lying. This is a matter of which we can never be certain.

After our long conversation that night I returned home alone. I knew that I had opened a wound in his soul. I had undermined his crumbling philosophy and the holes will grow more gaping with time. His weak logic will not be able to mend them.

I whispered a prayer for him hoping that his terror may yet save him; for when all paths for the entry of truth are barred with obstinacy fear may be the only path left.

I knew well that his guidance was not in my power. Didn't God say to His Prophet:

> "You do not guide whomever you will but God guides whomever He pleases"

But I hoped and prayed that my friend see the light of faith. There is no sin or fate worse than disbelief.

Fate and Predestination

Sheikh Mohammad M.
Al-Sha'rawi

In the Name of God the Most Merciful the Most Compassionate

Allah
The Divine Nature

Yassin Roushdy

THE SIGNS BEFORE THE DAY OF JUDGEMENT

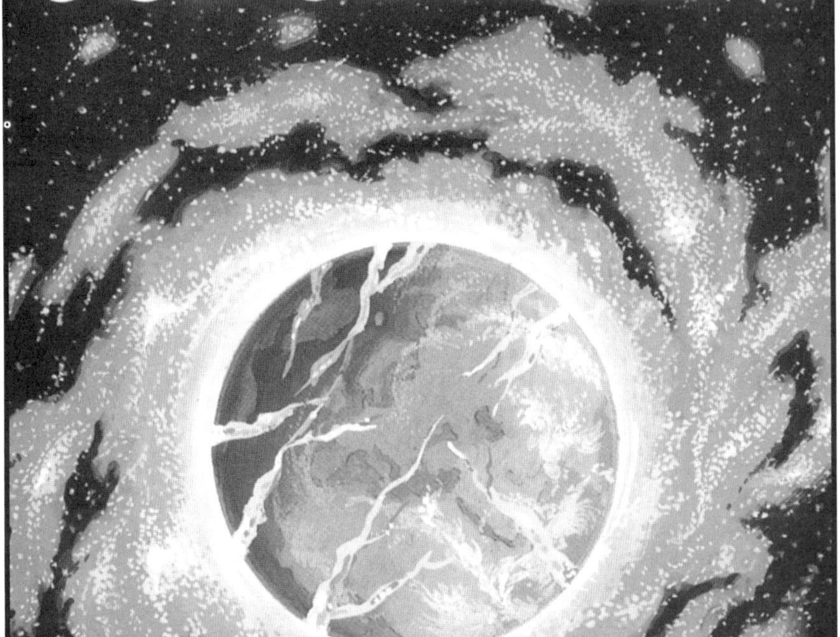

IBN KATHĪR

In the Name of God the Most
Merciful the Most Compassionate

AD-DUNYÃ

THE BELIEVER'S PRISON THE DISBELIEVER'S PARADISE

Muhammad 'Abd ar-Rahman 'Iwad

In the Name of God the Most
Merciful the Most Compassionate

MUHAMMAD

Peace and Blessing be upon Him

His Life, His Miracles, With His Companions

Dr. Mustafa Mahmoud
Translated by Niemat Ali Gadalla

The World of The Angels

Sheikh
'Abdu'l-Hamid
Kishk

In the Name of God the Most Merciful the Most Compassionate

Circumcision in Islam

Abu Bakr Abdu'r-Razzaq

THE ISRĀ' AND MI'RĀJ
THE PROPHET'S NIGHT-JOURNEY AND ASCENT INTO HEAVEN

'Abd-Allah Ḥajjāj